The Greatest Three-Way Rivalries in Sports History

James Simpson II

©2012 by James T. Simpson, II. All rights reserved.

All pictures were acquired from the Associated Press and Getty Images.

INTRODUCTION

As an avid sports fan, what can I say: I'M HOOKED. Have been hooked, still am hooked and will continue to be hooked (for better or worse). Where does the obsession come from? Heck, a number of things come to mind but the one aspect of sports that has drawn fans even more to the game, lifts sports to prodigious heights and hooks me the most is without a doubt...RIVALRIES! I'm staying off the subject of team rivalries and gearing my attention towards individual rivalries or as I like to call them, TWO-WAY RIVALRIES! When you think of the exceptional two-way rivalries that stand out throughout sports history, the obvious ones pop in your head: Ali-Frazier, Nicklaus-Palmer, Wilt-Russell, Magic-Bird, Manning-Brady, Evert-Navratilova, Agassi-Sampras, Federer-Nadal, Borg-McEnroe, Bradshaw-Staubach, Williams-DiMaggio, etc. Great list isn't it, although I want you to shift your attention – AGAIN -- to another type of rivalry that doesn't just include two players going at each other head-to-head...but involves three players. Remember the "Two-Way Rivalry" from earlier? Well, I'm bringing you the brand, spanking new, THREE-WAY RIVALRY! (I went with three-way rivalry over three-way triangle because it was more original, even though triangle sounds better.)

A rivalry is defined as a competition for the same objective or for superiority in the same field. Well, I like to define a "three-way rivalry" as "a fierce competition between three players in the same sport or field, that competed against one another, in the same league, during the same era, that played for different teams, who for at least a five-to-ten-year period seemed to always be brought up in numerous discussions and debates worldwide -- that when it came to the fans and the media -- the conversations were often enthusiastic, animated and non-stop." I have created a Top 10 list in reverse order that involves the greatest three-way rivalries in sports history. These are three of the all-time best at their sport, who constantly battled each other year-after-year for supremacy in their craft. Whether championships, individual accolades, respect, recognition, or just seeking alpha dog status came into play, there was always something important on the line in these matchups. When it came to these trios, the labels," Who's the best player in the league or in the sport?" or "Who's the best player at his/her position?" forever surrounded these athletes during their playing days and in the end, that's what made it special. To make things more interesting, at the end of each section, I ranked the players based on who I felt was better all-time and who got the better of the rivalry. With all that being said, let's jump to the list.

Honorable Mention

- **Alex Rodriguez-Derek Jeter-Nomar Garciaparra.** The three best shortstops in the American League during the late 1990s and early 2000s in a bright era at the position.

- **Martin Brodeur-Patrick Roy-Dominik Hasek.** When you think about the goalie position in hockey during the 1990s and 2000s, these three usually come to mind. Without a question, three of the top 10 goalkeepers to ever step foot on the ice.

- **Sandy Koufax-Bob Gibson-Juan Marichal.** Not only were they the three finest pitchers in the National League during the 1960s but the cream of the crop at that position in all of baseball during that time. Throughout their careers, each pitcher intimidated the daylights out of opponents, had devastating stuff and just plain overwhelmed batters in a way we've rarely seen since.

- **Greg Maddox-Roger Clemens-Randy Johnson.** With apologies to Pedro Martinez (my favorite pitcher ever), The Rocket (Clemens), Mad Dog (Maddox) and The Big Unit (Johnson), edge out Pedro (barely) as the top three elite pitchers of the 1990s. The three won a combined nine Cy Young awards throughout the decade. 'Nuff said.

The Greatest Individual Sports Rivalries in 3's

10. Troy Aikman-Brett Favre-Steve Young

They might not have been the three premier quarterbacks in the 1990s (John Elway, Dan Marino and Jim Kelly are the others that come to mind) but they were invariably brought up in the typical conversation as to, "Who's the top QB in football?" Most importantly each consistently had their team in title contention during the decade. When you're the quarterback of the Dallas Cowboys, Green Bay Packers and the San Francisco 49ers (three of the top five NFL franchises ever) your play is always scrutinized and the expectations are forever shooting through the roof, but when you deliver -- the fans are pretty much ready to build a statue of you. These three delivered. From 1992 to 1997, at least one of these three quarterbacks represented the NFC in the Super Bowl and in that six-year span they each led their teams to a Super Bowl title, with Aikman winning three, and Young and Favre one apiece. When it came to the playoffs, it seemed like every year each quarterback had to get pass the other one to reach The Big Game and it was true. THEY USUALLY DID.

1992: NFC Championship Game
#2 Cowboys def. #1 49ers, 30-20

This was the first of what would be three straight NFC title game clashes between Aikman's Cowboys and Young's 49ers. The 49ers marched into the title game having the best record in the league at 14-2, with the Cowboys holding the second best record at 13-3. If you watched both teams closely that season, any football fan with common sense could have told you those were clearly the two best teams in the game. Both quarterbacks played well but when it came down the stretch, Dallas' defense and Aikman made the critical plays to win on the road. A week later, Aikman would go on to win Super Bowl MVP as Dallas blasted the Buffalo Bills 52-17 to win their first Super Bowl title in 14 years. As for Favre, the Packers missed the playoffs in his first year as a starter.

EDGE: **AIKMAN**

**1993: NFC Divisional Playoff Game
#1 Cowboys def. #6 Packers, 27-17**

    **NFC Championship
#1 Cowboys def. #2 49ers, 38-21**

Playing in his second career playoff game, Favre and up-and-coming Green Bay were overmatched by the defending champs. Favre put up big numbers with 331 passing yards but the Aikman (28 of 37 passes completed, 302 passing yards) to Michael Irvin connection was too much on that day. In the NFC title game rematch, Dallas overwhelmed San Francisco. Dallas rattled Young all day and even when Aikman suffered a concussion early in the 3rd quarter, backup Bernie Kosar stepped in (as he did earlier in the season) and kept the momentum going. Dallas would again meet the Bills in the Super Bowl and again would walk away with another title.

EDGE: **AIKMAN**

**1994: NFC Divisional Playoff Game
#2 Cowboys def. #4 Packers, 35-9**

    **NFC Championship Game
#1 49ers def. #2 Cowboys, 38-28**

Dallas would again smash Green Bay in the divisional round. While Aikman clicked on all cylinders, Favre mightily struggled. In the offseason, San Francisco made some key free agent acquisitions bringing in former Cowboys linebacker Ken Norton Jr. and the top cornerback in the game, Deion Sanders to help overthrow the Cowboys. For the third straight year, the 49ers and Cowboys were set to battle with a Super Bowl berth on the line. Aikman was coming into the title game with a perfect 7-0 playoff record as a starter, while Young had the "Can't win the big game" label looming over him. With those big moves, the 1994 49ers proved to be one of the most prolific, all-around teams in NFL History and they showed it, as they finally conquered the Cowboys and then destroyed the Chargers 49-26 in the Super Bowl. By throwing a Super Bowl record six TD passes (still stands today), Young walked away with the game's MVP and at last "got the monkey off his back."

EDGE: **YOUNG**

1995: NFC Divisional Playoff Game
#3 Packers def. #2 49ers, 27-17

NFC Championship Game
#1 Cowboys def. #3 Packers, 38-27

Green Bay jumped on the defending champion 49ers early and often, as Favre (299 passing yards, 2 TD passes, 0 INTs) got the better of Young (328 passing yards, 0 TD passes, 2 INTS) in their first playoff matchup. The NFC title game turned out to be an exciting offensive shootout between the Packers and Cowboys, with Dallas sending the Pack home for the third consecutive year and on their way back into the Big Game. Favre and Green Bay proved they were equipped enough to be champs in the future, although the time wasn't now. Dallas would go on to capture their third Super Bowl title in four years and with that championship, they cemented themselves as a football dynasty. Aikman at the time would become only the third quarterback in history along with Joe Montana and Terry Bradshaw to win three Super Bowl rings or more in their career.

ANOTHER EDGE: **AIKMAN**

1996: NFC Divisional Playoff Game
#1 Packers def. #4 49ers, 35-14

Dallas' quest at a remarkable feat of winning four Super Bowl trophies in five years ended in the divisional round to the expansion Carolina Panthers. Dallas' reign atop the league was soon coming to a halt. While the Cowboys dynasty was fading, the Packers were looking to replace Dallas at the top of the NFC. On a rainy, muddy day at Lambeau, Favre and Green Bay did a number on Young's 49ers, who were also slowly waning from Super Bowl contention. The Packers would put "Titletown USA" back on the map by marching to the franchise's first Super Bowl title since 1967.

EDGE: **FAVRE**

1997: NFC Championship Game
#2 Packers def. #1 49ers, 23-10

Injuries and off-field incidents unsettled the Cowboys season as they missed the playoffs for the first time since 1990. The 49ers and Packers finished as the top two seeds in the NFC and met for the third straight year in the playoffs. Green Bay would knock out San Francisco and return to the Super Bowl as heavy favorites but would go down against John Elway and the wild-card Denver Broncos.

EDGE: **FAVRE**

**1998: NFC Wild Card Game
#4 49ers def. #5 Packers, 30-27**

All three teams were still playoff-caliber at this point but no longer Super Bowl contenders. The Cowboys would become upset victims by the young Arizona Cardinals in the wild card round. This was to be the fourth postseason in a row the Niners and Packers would slug it out. Favre had a 3-0 playoff record against his rival Young but Young would get the upper hand this time as he threw the game-winning TD pass with eight seconds remaining in one of the greatest NFL playoff finishes. The 49ers would later fall to the eventual NFC champion Atlanta Falcons in the divisional round.

EDGE: No one deserves to get the nod this season. I'm leaving this one **UNCLEAR**.

So, let's take a look at the QBs head-to-head playoff record against one another...

Aikman- 2-1 vs. Young, 3-0 vs. Favre

       5-1 combined record

Young- 1-2 vs. Aikman, 1-3 vs. Favre

       2-5 combined record

Favre- 0-3 vs. Aikman, 3-1 vs. Young

       3-4 combined record

And that leads us to this...

Preview of the 1994 NFC Championship Game.

Young and Favre sharing a moment.

Young finally capturing the Lombardi Trophy after Super Bowl XXIX.

Aikman and Favre shaking hands after doing battle.

The Old Gun Slinger running away from a Dallas defender during the 1995 NFC Championship Game.

The Cowboys "Big Three" of Aikman, Smith and Irvin.

So, Who's Better- The head-to-head playoff records are telling but not that convincing. The quarterbacks play was an important factor in these playoff games, given it was not always the tipping point. I always thought Aikman got the raw end of the stick from the media for playing with so much talent. Yeah, he did have a ton of talent surrounding him, but that doesn't always guarantee success. Aikman seized control of the team, showed he was a proven leader and maybe was the most accurate, decisive quarterback ever to play. Believe me, it wasn't a mistake Aikman led his team to 3 titles in 4 years. He was that good. After saying that, this is where the numbers and individual honors thing hurts Aikman and comes into play for Young and Favre. (By the way, if Dallas asked Aikman to throw more and carry a little more of the load, I believe his statistics could have been larger, yet they leaned strongly on one of the great offensive lines in history and one of the three best running backs ever in Emmitt Smith.) Brett Favre should be known as the Emperor of NFL Passing Records. He's the all-time leader in career: TD passes (508), interceptions (336), passing yards (71,838), completions (6,300), attempts (10,169), consecutive starts by a quarterback (297), regular season wins by a starting quarterback (186), seasons with at least 30 TD passes (9), seasons with at least 20 TD passes (15), most seasons with at least 3,000 passing yards (18), consecutive MVP awards (3) from 1995-1997 and the list keeps on going. When you think of Favre's legacy, you think of the passing records he holds. To me, Favre's the "Nolan Ryan of Football." The stats good or bad, pretty much define their careers and that's just not good enough when you're mentioned by many as the best QB of all-time. Favre did have a strong sense of the big moments during late game situations, but he lacked the leadership qualities that most great signal callers usually have and *should* have.

Is it me or is Steve Young the most underrated, great quarterback ever? He rarely gets mentioned with Unitas, Brady, Manning, Montana, Elway and Marino, but he should. His resume reads: Two NFL MVPs (1992,1994), one Super Bowl MVP, had the highest passer rating ever in a single season at 112.8 in 1994 (before Peyton Manning broke it in 2004 at 121.8, then Tom Brady in 2007 at 117.2, then again by Aaron Rodgers at 122.5 in 2011), the third best QB rating in history (96.8), the most career rushing TDs by a quarterback (43), most seasons with a passer rating over 100 (6), one of only four QBs to lead the league in touchdown passes 4 times tied with Johnny Unitas, Brett Favre, and Len Dawson, and an impressive and unappreciated six passing titles (tied with Sammy Bough with the most). Young's eight straight seasons of leading San Francisco to 10 wins or more goes unrecognized and his all-time QB ratio of 232 TD passes to 107 INTs get left in the dust when discussing his career. Not many quarterbacks produced the elusiveness, quickness and instincts he had as a runner, along with his skillful touch, scary deep ball and mastery accuracy. So, when we mention who we think are the top six or seven quarterbacks ever, why isn't Young's name brought up in the equation? My answer: Longevity. When you access his career, he was only great for six seasons. In the realm of things, that's an element that critics can hold against an athlete when discussing where they stand in history.

When it comes down to it, Favre was more consistently great, while Aikman was the better big game player and the best winner but Young was more of a complete player and could beat teams in more ways. Favre was too reticent, unpredictable and erratic as a quarterback to trust anything he did on the field, especially in big moments. With the aptitude of excellent teams Young played on, he should have won more than one Super Bowl as a starter (he won two as a backup behind Montana) but as much as you can't dismiss the fact that Aikman quarterbacked a football dynasty, he just wasn't the elite passer Young was. Steve Young had a rare quarterback skill set that set him apart from Favre and Aikman.

My Rankings

1. **Steve Young**
2. **Troy Aikman**
3. **Brett Favre**

9. Jack Nicklaus-Arnold Palmer-Gary Player

The self-proclaimed "Big Three of Golf". These three dominated the game from the late 1950s through the 1970s and made golf as alluring as the other major sports. Golf reached new heights in the early 1960s and the sport's popularity grew on millions of television sets, mainly because of Nicklaus, Palmer and Player. While the South African Player was making his presence known on the tour, Palmer recognized as "The King", was drawing new fans with his stimulating style and relaxed personality. He was the first golfer that was perceived as and carried himself as a superstar. The 1960s came and the arrival of the chubby, more talented, powerful Nicklaus would soon challenge Palmer for golfs top dominion. The 1960 U.S. Open was full evidence of how daunting the two-time U.S. Amateur champion would be, finishing second; two behind Palmer. The period where Nicklaus, Palmer and

Player were each at the top of the sport was from 1960-1966, where during that stretch they combined to win 15 major championships out of 29 (Palmer and Nicklaus each 6, Player 3) and in seven consecutive years at least one of them won The Masters. Talk about being in full command of the PGA Tour!

Along with the 1960 U.S. Open, the majors produced some celebrated battles between the three…

1961 Masters- Gary Player became the first international player to win at Augusta, winning by one stroke over Arnold Palmer and Charles Coe.

1962 Masters- Arnold Palmer would win his third Masters title by defeating Gary Player and Dow Finsterwald in the tournament's first three-way playoff.

1962 U.S. Open- Jack defeated Arnie in a remarkable 18-hole playoff to take his first major title. Jack ended up shooting a 71 to Arnie's 74 in the final round.

1964 Masters- What would be his fourth green jacket and seventh and final major, Arnold Palmer put on a wonderful show winning by six strokes over his rival Nicklaus and Dave Marr.

1965 Masters- Jack Nicklaus would go on to score a then-Masters record 17-under-par 271 to win his second green jacket. To make it more special, he defeated his two biggest rivals Player and Palmer by a resounding nine strokes. The Golden Bear was at the peak of his game.

1967 U.S. Open- Nicklaus would again get the best of Palmer in a highly-contested encounter, winning his seventh career major by four shots.

1968 British Open- Gary Player wins his second of three claret jugs by getting pass Nicklaus and Bob Charles by two shots.

As you can see, the Big 3 produced some excellent matchups and amazing golf that lifted the PGA Tour to relevancy and mainstream status.

The Old Timers taking a stroll on the course.

Arnie and Jack at the 1962 U.S. Open.

The Big Three of Golf posing together.

Chilling at Augusta National.

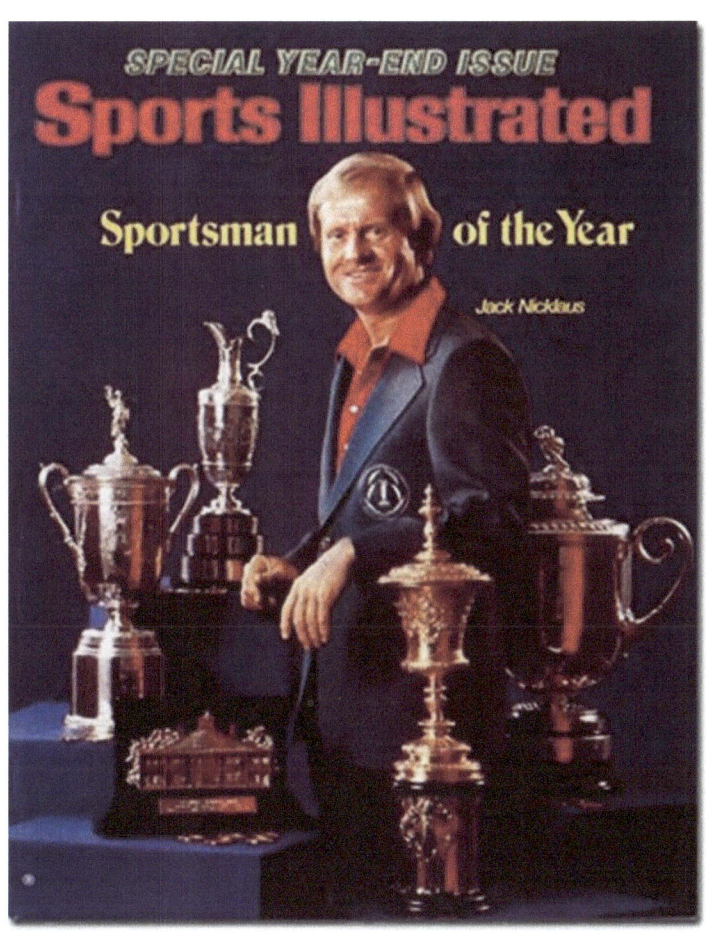

The Golden Bear won the 1978 Sports Illustrated Sportsman of the Year.

So, Who's Better- There are only five players in golf history that have won all four majors: Gene Sarazen, Ben Hogan, Tiger Woods, Gary Player and Jack Nicklaus. After I first saw the list, I asked myself, "Where's Arnold Palmer?" I thought it was a mistake, but no, he wasn't in the group and that kind of baffled me. For a player of Palmer's statue, who was one of the most revered athletes ever (In February 2011, he was named one of the 25 Coolest Athletes of all-time by *GQ Magazine* for crying out loud) and an exceptional golfer, I could not understand why he *only* won seven majors. When I assessed all three of their resumes, it is pretty self-explanatory who's the best.

Gary Player
PGA Player of the Year awards: 0
PGA Wins: 24 (T-25th of all-time)
Seasons leading the tour in wins: 0
Money list titles: 0
Major titles: 9, (T- 4th all-time)-3 Masters, 3 British Opens, 2 PGA Championships, 1 U.S. Open

Arnold Palmer
PGA Player of the Year awards: 2 (T-5th all-time)
PGA Wins: 62 (5th all-time)
Seasons led the tour in wins: 5 (T-3rd all-time)
Money list titles: 4 (4th all-time)
Major titles: 7 (T-7th all-time)-4 Masters, 2 British Opens, 1 U.S. Open

Jack Nicklaus
PGA Player of the Year awards: 5 (3rd all-time)
PGA Wins: 73 (T-2nd all-time)
Seasons led the tour in wins: 5 (T-3rd all-time)
Money list titles: 8 (2nd all-time)
Major titles: 18 (1st all-time)-6 Masters (1st all-time), 5 PGA Championships (T-1st all-time), 4 U.S. Opens (T-1st all-time), 3 British Opens (T-4th all-time)

After checking all that out, you do the math.

My Rankings

1. **Jack Nicklaus**
2. **Arnold Palmer**
3. **Gary Player**

8. Larry Bird-Magic Johnson-Julius Erving

If I said, Magic (my favorite player of all-time), Larry Legend and Dr. J were the three defining players in the NBA during the early/mid 1980s, would I possibly be wrong? Maybe. If you want to throw Kareem, Moses, Isiah, or Gervin in the mix, then I couldn't argue with you. Therefore, if you're talking about having a huge impact on the league and giving pro basketball an immense boost, then I think Larry Bird, Julius Erving and Magic Johnson were the three most important players during that period. Without a doubt in my mind. When the NBA-ABA merger went through in 1976 -- with Erving joining the NBA -- the Doctor soon blew fans away with his awesome hangtime ability, transcendent dunks, big Afro and composing style that the basketball world would elatedly gravitate towards. Magic and Bird arrived on the scene in 1979 and elevated the game to a new summit and changed the NBA forever. At a time when pro basketball was at a low point, these three stormed into the league and brought a level of flashiness, showmanship and creativity that glued millions to the TV set. They regularly had fans jumping out their seats after a, "Did you just see that play" type moment…and believe me, both Magic and Bird averaged like four or five of those moments a game.

The league not only benefited from these three superstars but also from their star-studded teams that ruled the NBA during the '80s. From 1980-1987, Bird's Celtics, Magic's Lakers (OK, it was Kareem's team too) and Erving's Sixers were the cream of the crop. Those seemed to be the only teams in the league that mattered. Every season those three were the main favorites and when playoff time came, they often had to beat one another in order to hoist the Larry O'Brien Trophy at the end of the year. In that eight year span, each year either the Celtics or Sixers won the Eastern Conference (Celtics five times, Sixers three times) and while they both rumbled through the East, the mighty Lakers were busy pulverizing through the Western Conference to make six finals in eight seasons. The Lakers faced the Celtics and Sixers each three times in the championship series during their six finals trips and each time the series generated a number of marvelous individual matchups, classic games and some of the most riveting, fantastic basketball the league has ever witnessed. To prove their dominance, the three teams combined to win 9 titles in 10 years throughout the '80s. That's called domination at its finest folks!

Let's take a look at each rivals head-to-head matchups over the decade...

Bird's Celtics vs. Erving's Sixers

Head-to-Head playoff series tied at 2-2

**1980 East Finals- #3 Sixers def. #1 Celtics, 4-1
1981 East Finals- #1 Celtics def. #3 Sixers, 4-3
1982 East Finals- #3 Sixers def. #1 Celtics, 4-3
1985 East Finals- #1 Celtics def. #3 Sixers, 4-1**

(Just too clear things up: Don't let the Sixers No.3 seed each of those years fool you. Each of those years except 1985, the Celtics and Sixers had the two best records in the East and were visibly the two best teams in the conference. At that time, there were two divisions in each conference and the two teams who won their division would usually automatically get one of the top 2 seeds in the playoffs, regardless if a team from the other division, that didn't win their division might have had a better record than a team who won their division. The thing is the Celtics and Sixers were in the same division, so let's say the Celtics have the best record in the East and get the 1 seed and the Sixers, who would usually finish second in the division and have the second-best record in the conference would be a 3 seed -- right behind the other division winner who would be a 2 seed. Now if the 3 seed had a better record than the 2 seed, they would get home-court advantage against them in the second round, if they faced off. Are you confused? Did you get all that? I know, can't believe I wrote pretty much a paragraph explaining that. Where's David Stern when you need him? OK, let's just move on.)

The Boston-Philly series were titanic battles and Erving and Bird were at the forefront of the rivalry. The most memorable series between the two were by far in '81 and '82. During the 1981 NBA season, Boston and Philly separated themselves from the rest of the pack. They each tied for the league's best record at 62-20 and in the closest MVP race in NBA history up to that point, Erving and Bird finished 1-2. The 1981 Eastern Conference Finals between the two turned out to be not only one of the best playoff series of all-time (some even say the best) but also one of the great playoff comebacks. The seven-game war constructed five games that were decided by two points or fewer and after being down 3-1, Boston stormed back to win the series. Bird got the better of the league's MVP in the series averaging 27 pts-13 rebs-5 asts to Erving's 20 pts-6 rebs-4 asts and just maybe proved he deserved the MVP over Erving. The next year, the Sixers held a 3-1 series edge against the Celtics, only to have Bird & Co. comeback to tie the series at 3-3, just like they did a year ago. This time Philly would prevail by winning Game 7 in Boston Garden behind masterful performances by Dr. J and Andrew Toney.

Even though Boston and Philly split their playoff series at two apiece -- to me -- Boston got the better of the rivalry because of their 3 titles to Philly's 1 during the '80s and you can't forget the fact that they were greater for a longer period of time. Another way to look at it is: If you took each team's best squad from that era, the '83 Sixers and '86 Celtics (two of the top ten NBA teams ever) and had them go head-to-head, Who would you pick in a seven-game series? I'm taking the '86 Celtics. They were a once in a lifetime team. That's the icebreaker!

Magic's Lakers vs. Erving's Sixers

Lakers won head-to-head series 2-1

1980 NBA Finals- #1 Lakers def. #3 Sixers, 4-2
1982 NBA Finals- #1 Lakers def. #3 Sixers, 4-2
1983 NBA Finals- #1 Sixers def. #1 Lakers, 4-0

The 1980 NBA Finals was pitted as "Kareem vs. Dr. J" and they did not disappoint, but the Rookie of the Year runner-up Magic Johnson (You guessed it, behind Larry Bird) stole the show in Game 6. Playing all five positions, Magic had a legendary performance, tossing up a 42 pts-15 rebs-7 asts-3 stls game (with league MVP Kareem sitting out with an injury) to help the Lakers clinch the title. The 1982 season was almost a historic one for Magic when he averaged 18.6 pts, 9.6 rebs, 9.5 asts per game, becoming the closest player ever to average a triple-double since Oscar Robertson accomplished the feat in 1962. (To this day, when the sports public brings up the greatest individual seasons in NBA history, no one ever mentions Magic's 1982 season. They bring up Oscar in 1962, Wilt in 1962, Kareem in 1971, Jordan in 1996, Bird in 1986, Shaq in 2000, or Kobe in 2006, but never Magic in 1982. If you round it off the guy pretty much averaged a triple-double and it was one of the best all-around seasons of all-time by a player. How does it get overlooked? It's beyond me). In the wake of Magic's 16 pts-10 rebs-8 asts Finals MVP series average, the Lakers captured the '82 title, but Philly would come back in '83 led by newly acquired center and league MVP, Moses Malone to snatch the title. After falling short in three previous Finals trips in 1977, 1980 and 1982, Doc (19 pts-8 rebs-5 asts averages in '83 Finals) finally got his ring.

Magic's Lakers vs. Bird's Celtics

Lakers won head-to-head series 2-1

1984 NBA Finals- #1 Celtics def. #1 Lakers, 4-3
1985 NBA Finals - #1 Lakers def. #1 Celtics, 4-2
1987 NBA Finals- #1 Lakers def. #1 Celtics, 4-2

Memorable. Unforgettable. Significant. These are just some of the words to describe those Bird-Magic/Lakers-Celtics series. Before both players faced off in 1984, basketball fans, CBS and the league yearned for the chance to see these two transcendent stars battle each other on pro basketball's biggest stage. In their fifth season, they finally got their wish and it groomed to be something truly special. In my opinion, the 1984 Finals were not only the greatest playoff series ever but also the greatest Finals ever. You couldn't ask for anything better! You had the two best players in the game (Magic and Bird), the two best teams, the two greatest franchises, eight future Hall of Famers (Bird, Magic, Kareem, McHale, Parish, Worthy, McAdoo, and DJ), five other players who were all-star caliber (Cooper, Maxwell, Scott, Wilkes, Ainge), five quality role players (Rambis, M.L. Carr, Henderson, McGee, Wedman) and not to mention it was one of the most watched and famous playoff series of all-time.

The Boston-L.A. face-offs were so appealing that it attracted non-basketball fans to the TV screen and forced you to pick a side: Who you rolling with, Magic or Larry? (The Bird-Johnson rivalry is reminiscent of many of the exalted and fantastic individual music/acting/political debates of the last 60 years: Biggie or Tupac, Dr. King or Malcolm X, Jay-Z or Nas, Whitney or Mariah, Pacino or De Niro, Brando or Dean, Damon or DiCaprio, Britney or Christina, Prince or Michael Jackson, etc. A crazy good list. All those debates are just too close to call. They're each neck and neck. If you had to choose who you thought was better, who would you take? I know, can't decide, huh? You could pick one over the other and still not be fully convinced you made the right choice. Like the Bird-Johnson rivalry, as time goes by, these arguments will only get more gripping and enthralling by the minute). The rivalry was contagious and the fact that one was white and the other was black intrigued hoop fans even more. The league was invigorated and basketball was never more popular. There hasn't been a better individual rivalry in the NBA since.

Rocking the sports cards in the early '80s.

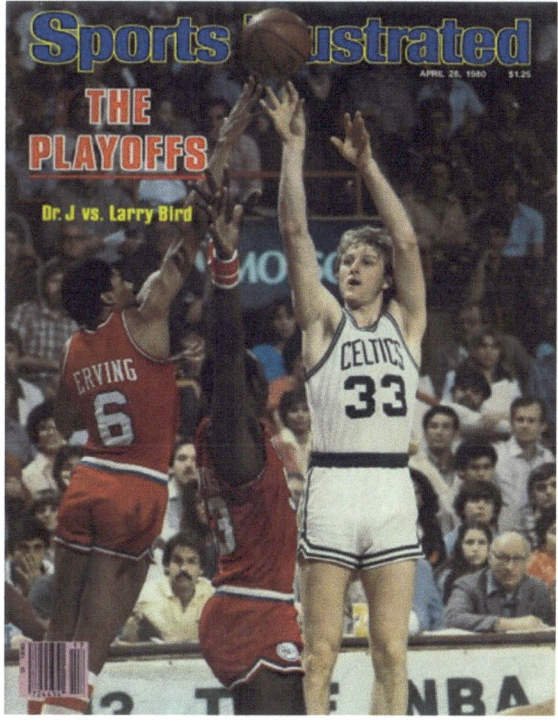

Bird shooting over Erving in the 1980 Eastern Conference Finals.

The Doctor gliding for a finger roll.

Magic and his partner in crime, Kareem Abdul-Jabbar.

These two were in a serious brawl in 1984.

Let's just say it got ugly.

The two greats paying close attention to the rim.

So, Who's Better- If someone asked me to describe Magic Johnson, Larry Bird and Julius Erving briefly, my response would be:

Magic Johnson was like an action-packed wizard on the court, who was always digging up an abundance of magic tricks up his sleeve to keep the crowd delighted.

Larry Bird was a diligent, crafty artist whose work could sometimes be elegant or sometimes messy but always effective and decisive.

Julius Erving was a cool, smooth operator who conducted through the air, by flying and gliding effortlessly to the amazement of millions.

As you can see, entertainment is what these three seamlessly brought to the game but it didn't define them, at least not for Magic and Bird. When people think about Dr. J, they fancy how he was a pioneer to the game, the great dunker he was and how fun it was to watch him play. That's honestly what people think. With Magic and Bird -- Champion, Competitor, Leader, Clutch and yes, entertaining comes to mind. Yes, Dr. J was a champion but not to the extent that Magic and Bird was. Magic Johnson and Larry Bird are defined as champions and most importantly *wanted* to be defined as champions. Dr. J wanted to win, but not as badly as those two. What Dr. J lacked was the willingness and understanding to do everything necessary his team needed from him in order to get the job done. Bird and Magic *knew* and *understood* that and they delivered. Plus, I've always thought NBA Dr. J (1976-1987) was a little overrated. The media built him up and was so animated by his dazzling dunks, that they seemed to forget that being a great player was more than just jumping from the free throw line and slamming on opponents. ABA Dr. J (1971-1976) was way better…and it's not even close. This three-way debate really comes down to "The Hick from French Lick" and "The King of Showtime"… and believe me, this was difficult. We have the greatest point guard ever, the greatest small forward ever and two of the five best all-around players ever to lace em' up. In current ESPN columnist Bill Simmons book titled "The Book of Basketball," he said when figuring out who was better all-time -- his tipping point was that Magic had twelve transcendent years compared to Bird's nine transcendent years -- so that pushed Magic over Bird, by a hair in his eyes.

My tipping point -- I think Magic was greater because he did a better job carrying the Lakers for his entire career than Bird did carrying the Celtics. They each led their squads to six 60-win seasons but Magic averaged 59 wins a season during his 12-year career compared to Bird averaging 57 wins a season in his 13-year career. Magic won five titles to Birds three. Magic made the Finals nine times to Birds five. Magic won back-to-back titles (1987 and 1988), while Bird never won consecutive titles. Most importantly, Magic was 2-1 against Bird in the Finals, plus if you count the 1979 National Championship Game between the two that Magic won, then his record turns to 3-1 overall versus Bird in championship series/title games. That's what swung it for me.

My Rankings

1. **Magic Johnson**
2. **Larry Bird**
3. **Julius Erving**

7. Chris Evert-Martina Navratilova-Steffi Graf

Probably the three greatest female tennis players ever.

Chris Evert was the American beauty that played the game with wonderful balance and grace. With her trademark two-handed backhand, she possessed tenacious passing shots in her arsenal that made her opponents think twice about coming to the net.

Martina Navratilova was the "physically, stronger than anyone else on tour lefty" who towered over the women's game with her powerful serve and volley approach.

Steffi Graf was an expertise, complete, all-court player with no holes in her game: she served well, sliced well, volleyed well, moved well, had top-notch athleticism, had an excellent forehand, excellent backhand, and could beat you with offense and defense.

The three of them had such a deliberate command over women's tennis and were so superior against their opponents that it's hard to comprehend exactly how dominant they were, unless I throw these incredible numbers at you…

Most Grand Slam Finals since the Open Era (1968)
1. Chris Evert- 34
2. Martina Navratilova- 32
3. Steffi Graf- 31

Most Grand Slam Titles won
1. Margaret Court- 24
2. Steffi Graf- 22
3. Helen Willis Moody- 19
4. Chris Evert- 18
4. Martina Navratilova- 18

Most Singles Titles of All-Time
1. Martina Navratilova- 167
2. Chris Evert- 154
3. Steffi Graf- 107

Most Consecutive WTA Singles Titles won
1. Martina Navratilova- 13 (1984)
2. Margaret Court- 12 (1972-1973)
3. Steffi Graf- 11 (1989-1990)
4. Chris Evert- 10 (1974)

Most Consecutive Years winning at least one singles title
1. Martina Navratilova- 21 (1974-1994)
2. Chris Evert- 18 (1971-1988)
3. Steffi Graf- 14 (1986-1999)

Women's All-Time Career Winning Percentage
1. Margaret Court- 593-56, 91.3%
2. Chris Evert- 1,304-144, 90.3%
3. Steffi Graf- 900-115, 88.6%
4. Martina Navratilova- 1,442-219, 86.8%

Most Singles Matches Won All-Time
1. Martina Navratilova- 1,442 wins
2. Chris Evert- 1,304 wins

3. Steffi Graf- 900 wins

Most Consecutive Grand Slam Singles Titles won
1. Martina Navratilova- 6 (1983-1984), T-1st all-time
2. Steffi Graf- 5 (1988-1989)
3. Steffi Graf- 4 (1993-1994), T-3rd all-time
4. Chris Evert- 3 (1982-1983), T-4th all-time
4. Steffi Graf- 3 (1989-1990, 1995, 1996), T-4th all-time

Most Consecutive Grand Slam Finals
1. Steffi Graf- 13 (1987-1990)
2. Martina Navratilova- 11 (1985-1987)
3. Martina Navratilova- 6 (1983-1984)
3. Chris Evert- 6 (1984-1985)

Most Consecutive Weeks at No.1
1. Steffi Graf- 186
2. Martina Navratilova- 156
3. Chris Evert- 113

Total Weeks at No.1
1. Steffi Graf- 377
2. Martina Navratilova- 332
3. Chris Evert- 260

Most Times ended the year at No.1
1. Steffi Graf- 8
2. Martina Navratilova- 7
3. Chris Evert- 5

- Best Women's Clay Court Singles Winning Percentage of All-Time-
  Chris Evert- 316-20, 94.0%

- Best Women's Hard Court Singles Winning Percentage of All-Time-
  Steffi Graf- 335-36, 90.3%

- Best Women's Grass Court Singles Winning Percentage of All-Time-

    Martina Navratilova- 305-39, 88.6%

- Best Women's Carpet Court Singles Winning Percentage of All-Time-

    Martina Navratilova- 516-58, 89.9%

    (Didn't know they played on carpet, now did you?)

- From 1975 to 1990, either Evert, Graf, or Navratilova finished the year ranked No.1 in the world.

Holy Moly! Talk about three players having a threshold over a sport! In the majority of all those categories: 1-2-3 finishes amongst the three. Crazy! During their careers, Navratilova, Evert and Graf were the Queens of Women's Tennis, while the rest of the field was bowing down to them as its subjects. So you ask -- Why are they only 7 on the list? Because the rivalry between the three only lasted a few years (1985-1989), when each player was in their prime or still in top form. It just didn't last long enough to move up on the list but doesn't mean it wasn't must-see tennis. Up into 1985, the Evert-Navratilova rivalry had been going on for about a decade. They were the alpha dogs in women's tennis and there were no signs of anyone dethroning them... until Graf came along. Graf turned pro in 1982, although 1985 was the year she emerged as a serious threat to Evert and Navratilova -- making the '85 U.S. Open semifinals, only to lose to Navratilova in straight sets (6-2, 6-3). During 1985, Evert and Navratilova faced each other in three Grand Slam Finals: Navratilova would beat Evert at the Australian Open and Wimbledon final, while Evert won at the French Open final.

In an impressive stretch starting at the 1986 French Open to the 1988 U.S. Open, Graf, Evert, and Navratilova would be the top 3 seeds in eight Grand Slam tournaments out of eleven. While the Australian Open was canceled in 1986, Navratilova and Evert still continued their reign atop women's tennis, with Evert defeating Navratilova (2-6, 6-3, 6-3) at the French Open final -- which was the 18th and final major of her career. Navratilova went on to win Wimbledon, the U.S. Open, and ended the year at No.1 for the fifth year in a row. It would be her final year holding the top spot. 1987 proved to be Graf's breakout year. With Evert starting to slow down, Graf and Navratilova would soon begin to establish a new rivalry in women's tennis. In the 1987 French Open final, Graf defeated No.1

Navratilova (6-4, 4-6, 8-6) in a thrilling three-setter to win her first Grand Slam title. At Wimbledon, Navratilova defeated Evert in the semifinals (6-2, 5-7, 6-4), then returned the favor, taking out Graf in the final (7-5, 6-3). The two battled again -- this time at the U.S. Open final -- with Navratilova winning her fourth U.S. Open title; but Graf finished the year at No.1, building on what would be an historical season the following year for the young German.

In 1988, Graf completed most likely the greatest season in women's and men's tennis history. Graf became the third woman (Maureen Connolly in 1953, Margaret Court in 1970) to win the Calendar Year Grand Slam (winning all four majors in the same year) and she added to her magnificent season by winning a gold medal at the women's single tournament at the '88 Summer Olympic Games. The media called this "The Golden Grand Slam." All at the age of 19! It hasn't been duplicated since and most likely never will. On her way to the Grand Slam that year, Graf bested Evert in the Aussie Open final (6-1, 7-6 (7-3)) and ended Navratilova's streak of six consecutive Wimbledon titles in the final (5-7, 6-2, 6-1). In 1989, Graf continued to soar -- winning three out of the four Slams, defeating Navratilova in the Wimbledon and U.S. Open final.

Evert retired in 1989; Navratilova past her prime would still be competitive for a few more years -- winning one more slam (1990 Wimbledon) before she walked away from singles competition in 1994 and Graf sustained to be the top player in the world well into the 1990s (Graf had a fabulous rivalry with Monica Seles in the early-to-mid '90s), winning 14 Grand Slams throughout the decade.

Let's take a look at each player's head-to-head meetings from 1985-1989:

<u>Chris Evert</u>
6-8 vs. **Graf**
1-2 vs. Graf in Grand Slam matches
0-1 vs. Graf in Grand Slam Finals

7-12 vs. **Navratilova**
3-5 vs. Navratilova in Grand Slam matches
2-2 vs. Navratilova in Grand Slam Finals

-Won 2 Grand Slam titles

<u>Martina Navratilova</u>
12-7 vs. **Evert**
5-3 vs. Evert in Grand Slam matches
2-2 vs. Evert in Grand Slam Finals

9-9 vs. **Graf**
5-4 vs. Graf in Grand Slam matches
2-4 vs. Graf in Grand Slam Finals

-Won 6 Grand Slam titles

<u>Steffi Graf</u>
8-6 vs. **Evert**
2-1 vs. Evert in Grand Slam matches
1-0 vs. Evert in Grand Slam Finals

9-9 vs. **Navratilova**
4-5 vs. Navratilova in Grand Slam matches
4-2 vs. Navratilova in Grand Slam Finals

-Won 8 Grand Slam titles

We see Graf during that five-year span had a slightly better run than Evert and Navratilova. Which leads us to this question...

Martina and Chrissie back in the mid-to-late '70s.

Two hard-hitting ladies in the late 1980s.

Navratilova and Evert both holding the French Open trophy.

Graf hoisting the 1988 Wimbledon crown.

Martina owned Wimbledon like no other woman.

The American and the Czech posing for a picture

before their classic 1984 U.S. Open Final.

Steffi with the forceful forehand.

So, Who's Better- This is going to be tricky. Evert was the best on the slow courts (clay). Navratilova was the best on the fast courts (grass). Graf flourished on all surfaces. Graf won each slam four times or more (7 Wimbledons, 6 French Opens, 5 U.S. Opens, 4 Australian Opens). Navratilova and Evert can't say that. Does that push Steffi pass Chrissie and Martina? It could. Navratilova won a major in three different decades (1970s, 1980s, and 1990s). Graf and Evert didn't accomplish that. What about Evert winning a record of at least one grand slam title for 13 consecutive years (1974-1986)? Her two rivals didn't achieve that feat. Dang, these ladies were doing their thang on the tennis courts! This gets tougher.

The Graf-Evert rivalry is difficult to judge. Evert won the first six matches, then Graf reeled off eight straight to finish 8-6 all-time vs. Evert. While Graf's game started peaking in 1987-1988, Evert's game started slipping and that's when Graf got the best of her. Can we really judge who's better between the two when most of their matches featured one player who was in their prime and the other was still formidable, but past their prime? Yes and No. Could 1980 Evert beat 1988 Graf, taken that players in 1988 were playing a more diverse style of tennis, using different equipment/rackets, hitting the ball harder, were stronger, more athletic and faster than players in 1980? Possibly, but we really don't know. This is where I draw the line. Graf had a better career than Evert and won the head-to-head battles. I'll give Graf the edge barely.

What about the Navratilova-Evert rivalry? In the first half of their career, Evert posted a 25-8 record against Navratilova from March 1973 to June 1979, when Evert was ruling the women's game and Navratilova had yet to peak. Navratilova would soon turn her fortune -- going 35-12 vs. Evert from June 1979 to November 1988 in the second half of their career and at one point Navratilova won 13 straight matches against Evert between 1982-1984, when she was at her pinnacle. Chrissie was better the first half of their rivalry; Martina was better in the second half. Martina posted a 43-37 all-time record against Chrissie, including a 10-4 mark in Grand Slam finals and a 14-8 edge overall in Grand Slam matches. The fact is: Navratilova was better than Evert all-time. Navratilova and Graf were just more dominant than Evert. This comes down to Martina and Steffi.

I came upon an interesting stat about the two. Did you know of the eight best win-loss records and winning percentage for a single season in women's tennis history that Graf and Navratilova each had four seasons apiece in the top eight? Here's the list:

1. Navratilova (1983)- 86-1, 98.9%

2. Graf (1989)- 86-2, 97.7%

3. Navratilova (1984)- 78-2, 97.5%

4. Graf (1987)- 75-2, 97.4%

5. Navratilova (1982)- 90-3, 96.8%

6. Navratilova (1986)- 89-3, 96.7%

7. Graf (1988)- 72-3, 96.0%

8. Graf (1995)- 47-2, 95.9%

(Note: Evert's best season was in 1978, with a 56-3 record and a 94.9% winning percentage, which ranked 10th all-time.)

Quite astonishing! As you can see, Navratilova posted the best record in women's history at 86-1 in 1983, while Graf had the second-best record at 86-2 in 1989. They finished 9-9 against each other all-time. Man, this debate couldn't get any harder! This is where I think Graf separates herself. Even though Graf was 4-5 vs. Navratilova in Grand Slam matches throughout their careers, she finished 4-2 versus Navratilova in Grand Slam finals -- including winning the last three. When they were both quintessential No.1 and No.2 in the world and both were enjoying their prime, Graf got the better of Navratilova, barely. I also think Graf is the most complete women's player ever, the greatest all-surface performer, and let's not forget she won 22 Slams to Navratilova and Evert's 18. At gunpoint...

My Rankings

1. **Steffi Graf**
2. **Martina Navratilova**
3. **Chris Evert**

6. Joe DiMaggio-Ted Williams-Stan Musial

"The Yankee Clipper", "The Splendid Splitter" and "Stan the Man" were the three prominent baseball players in the World War-II era of the 1940s. In that decade, games were played during the day, fans were constantly glued to the radio engaged by the action, and baseball was by far and away the premiere sport in our country -- becoming wildly admired by youths and even more attractive to the older generation. Joe DiMaggio was called the "Perfect Yankee." He was quiet, to himself, a dignified individual, disciplined, graceful and a serene player. Ted Williams was a dedicated student of hitting. Williams loved hitting, studied hitting, practiced hitting, challenged himself at hitting and wanted to be known as "The Greatest Hitter Who Ever Lived"... and to millions today, he is. Stan Musial was a consistently great, mildly undervalued, beloved figure, whose cheerful personality shined bright in baseball craze town, St. Louis for 22 seasons.

DiMaggio, Williams and Musial were the centerfaces of baseball in the '40s. Musial was the best player in the National League for a decade, while DiMaggio and Williams slugged it out year-after-year for the top spot in the American League. DiMaggio made his debut in 1936, and contributed immediately hitting .323 with 29 homers, scoring 132 runs, and 125 RBIs. With the help of the other Yankees star, Lou Gehrig, DiMaggio would carry the Yanks to four straight World Series titles from 1936-1939 and win the AL MVP in '39. That's one hell of a first four years in the majors, I can tell you that! Williams burst onto the scene in 1939 and was the most hyped rookie since, you guessed it...DiMaggio. Williams didn't disappoint -- hitting .327 with 31 homers, 145 RBIs and became the first rookie to lead the league in RBIs. Musial would make his entrance late in the 1941 season helping the surging Cardinals just miss chasing down the eventual National League champion Brooklyn Dodgers by 2 ½ games.

The 1941 baseball season would become one of the most historic and illustrious seasons in sports history and all eyes were on "Joltin Joe" and "Teddy Ballgame". Williams and DiMaggio would both have record breaking seasons. Williams reached the rare milestone of batting .400 in a single season with a .406 average (last player to bat .400 in a season) and DiMaggio produced a major league record 56-game hitting streak (that still stands today). Throughout the season, the two appeared to be in a back-and-forth, mano-a-mano contest to see who could grab the voter's attention and capture the AL MVP. They were jockeying for frontrunner status and the baseball globe couldn't have been more enlightened.

Let's take a look at both players' numbers in 1941...

Ted Williams- .406 batting average (1st), 37 HRs (1st), 120 RBIs (5th), 135 runs scored (1st), .553 on-base percentage (1st), .735 slugging percentage (1st)

Joe DiMaggio- .357 batting average (3rd), 30 HRs (5th), 125 RBIs (1st), 122 runs scored (2nd), .440 on-base percentage (3rd), .643 slugging percentage (2nd)

Looking at the numbers, Who do you think should be the AL MVP? Williams, right? I mean he was first in five out of six major statistical categories in the American League. Nope. DiMaggio walked away with the trophy with 291 votes to Williams 254 votes. DiMaggio was well-deserving, still I can't help but to think Williams was kind of robbed. Two things in my mind factored in that hurt Williams:

1.) Winning plays a key component too. The Yankees won 101 games and won the AL by 17 games over the 2nd place Red Sox. They would go on to win their fifth title in six years.

2.) The media was highly thoughtful of DiMaggio, while Williams' uneven relationship with the press and Boston fans might have hurt his chances at the winning the award.

Honestly, maybe it came down to the voters deciding which player's feat was more impressive. DiMaggio's 56-game winning streak or Williams .406 average? To me, its DiMaggio's streak. At the time, we've seen a player bat .400 before but we have never seen anything like DiMaggio's streak before, plus there's a slim possibility someone might bat .400 again. No one's ever touching Joe-Ds streak.

With the World War II approaching, 1942 would be the first season an infinite number of baseball players would begin to leave their teams to serve in the military. Williams and DiMaggio would leave to fight for their country in 1943, but in the meantime, they continued their high-level performance. Williams (.356 average, 36 HRs, 137 RBIs) won the 1942 Triple Crown and finished runner-up in the AL MVP race behind Yankees second baseman Joe Gordon, although he would be watching DiMaggio play in another World Series. In Musial's (.315 average, 72 RBIs, 10 triples, 32 doubles, 147 hits) first full season, he would lead his 106-win Cardinals past DiMaggio's (.305 average, 21 HRs, 114 RBIs) 103-win Yankees in the Fall Classic 4 games to 1. With Williams and DiMaggio off to the military for three seasons, Musial began to put himself at the top of baseballs headlines. Musial won the 1943 NL MVP, leading the National League in batting average at .357, triples at 20, doubles at 48, hits with 220, total bases with 437, on-base percentage at .425, slugging percentage at .562, and carried the Cardinals back to the World Series -- only to fall to the DiMaggio-less Yankees in 5 games.

The following year, Musial led St. Louis to its second title in three years, and then in 1945, Musial entered the U.S. Navy and missed the entire season. Williams, DiMaggio and Musial each rejoined their teams in 1946 and wouldn't miss a single beat. DiMaggio (.290 average, 25 HRs, 95 RBIs) had another All-Star season, but not quite at the level Williams and Musial did. Williams (.342 average, 38 HRs, 123 RBIs) and Musial (.365 average, 103 RBIs, 50 doubles, 20 triples, 228 hits) would each win their respective leagues MVP award and meet against each other in the Fall Classic. This was Williams' first and only World Series trip and it would end in disheartened fashion. In a tense seven-game series, St. Louis prevailed past Boston, winning a climatic game 7 at home 4-3. Williams struggled for most of the series, while Musial claimed his third World Series title in five years. During the 1947 season, the bulk of the focus was centered on the Brooklyn Dodgers new second baseman, Jackie Robinson, who became the first African-American to play in the major leagues, yet 1947 also served as the year the Ted Williams-Joe DiMaggio rivalry went up a notch. Williams won his second Triple Crown, joining Roger Hornsby as the only two players in history to win the Triple Crown twice. MVP season, right? It appeared to be but once again Williams was the next best person to DiMaggio -- losing by one point.

1947 Regular Season numbers

Ted Williams- .343 average (1st), 32 HRs (1st), 114 RBIs (1st), 125 runs scored (1st) .499 on-base percentage (1st), .634 slugging percentage (1st)

Joe DiMaggio- .315 average (7th), 20 HRs (6th), 97 RBIs (3rd), 97 runs scored (5th), .391 on-base percentage (8th), .522 slugging percentage (2nd)

"Teddy Ballgame" was first in all six of those categories. How does he not win the award? Totally unbelievable! DiMaggio won his third MVP crown and lifted the Yankees to another World Series title. Just when you thought the Williams-DiMaggio confrontation reached its height, the masterful 1949 AL pennant race famously called the "Summer of

'49" between DiMaggio's mighty Yankees and Williams' determined Red Sox added another chapter to the rivalry. With the Yankees and Red Sox going toe-to-toe all season, both teams heavily depended on its two superstars. The aging DiMaggio missed half of the season but returned and spurred the Yankees down the stretch. Williams with his brash confidence was clicking on all cylinders and helped put the Sox in the right position come season end. At season's end, Boston and New York's record was tied at 96-57 and this saga would all come down to the last game of the year between the two clubs. In an immensely anticipated game at Yankee Stadium, the Yankees clinched the pennant with a 5-3 win and later picked up another ring. 1951 was DiMaggio's last season and he would go out on top winning his ninth title and end one of the most decorated careers in baseball history. As the 1950s approached, Williams and Musial continued playing at an All-Star level (with Williams missing most of the '52 and '53 season due to flying combat missions in the Korean War) but none of them quite reached the immortal status and was the stellar player they were during the 1940s.

The 1940s were owned by none other than these three.

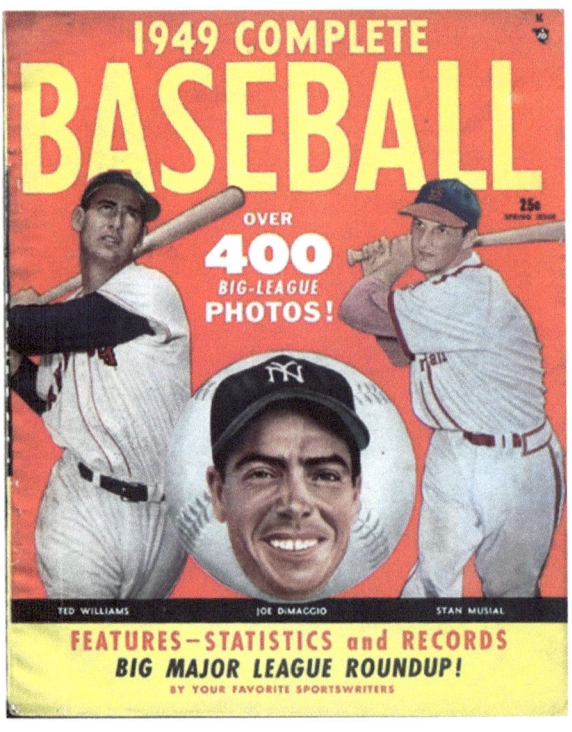

Nice pics!

An iconic photo.

Two of the most feared hitters ever.

Musial always seemed to have something to smile about.

The Debate that will never end.

So, Who's Better- Ted Williams was certainly the best offensive player of the three. Joe DiMaggio was the best all-around player. Stan Musial proved to be the most consistent player for a longer period of time. (Musial played in a record 24 All-Star games, tied with Willie Mays.)

If you want to discuss winning, DiMaggio owned that category.

DiMaggio- 9 championships, 10 pennants
Musial-   3 championships, 4 pennants
Williams- 0 championships, 1 pennant

When you look at the top 10 or 15 greatest position players ever (non-pitchers), DiMaggio might have been the best champion of them all. He personified what winning was all about and gave it his all everytime he stepped on the field. That counts for something, even if his teams were constantly loaded every year. Musial filled the stat sheet up in more categories year-after-year maybe more than any player in history. His 1948 MVP season, where he led the NL in 10 different categories (extra-base hits, total bases, slugging percentage, batting average, hits, on-base percentage, runs, doubles, triples, RBIs) remains as one of the great slept-on seasons the game has ever seen. When I think about Williams, not only does the immense number of notable nicknames he had -- "The Kid", "The Splendid Splinter", The Thumper", "Teddy Ballgame", "Mr. Red Sox", "Toothpick Ted", and "The Greatest Hitter Who Ever Lived" -- come to mind; nevertheless, the reality that he was a more dominant player than Musial and DiMaggio and could have had a much greater career than what he had, makes him kind of an unfinished creation. We can't forget the fact that Williams missed five seasons due to serving in the military. If he played those five seasons, he most likely gets to 700 HRs and it's not far-fetched to believe he would have eclipsed Babe Ruth's all-time homerun record. It's still mind-blowing to me that Williams didn't win MVP in his two Triple Crown seasons (1942, 1947). That would have taken him to another level historically.

The problem with Williams legacy was he never won, but was that solely his fault? I mean, yeah, DiMaggio's Yankees did always beat Williams' Red Sox, although the thing is: DiMaggio's Yankees beat *everyone*. They were so far and away better than every team that it was just silly. No matter how close Williams would get to DiMaggio, he wasn't beating that guy. Maybe he would outperform him but he wasn't defeating the dude. The Williams-DiMaggio rivalry reminds me a lot of the Wilt Chamberlain-Bill Russell rivalry. Like Williams, Chamberlain put up astronomical numbers and was the greater individual talent/player but like DiMaggio, Russell always had more talent surrounding him, beat his biggest rival constantly, and again and again won dozens of championships. Ted and Wilt were looked upon as being all about their statistics and failures, while Joe-D and Russell were viewed as distinguished leaders and the ultimate winners. Baseball is different than other sports like basketball and football. Star players can impact and change the outcome of the game more in those sports than in baseball, mainly because they get more opportunities and possessions to do so. For that, I can't put all of the blame on Williams for never getting Boston over the hump.

Here's some of the numbers and accomplishments in each players career:

Williams

2 AL MVPS
6 Batting titles
4 HR titles
4 RBI titles
12 times led league in On-base Percentage
9 times led league in Slugging Percentage
2 times led league in Doubles
6 times led league in Runs Scored
6 times led league in Total Bases
0 times led league in Triples
5 times led league in Extra-base hits

Musial

3 NL MVPS
7 Batting titles
0 HR titles
2 RBI titles
6 times led league in On-base Percentage
6 times led league in Slugging Percentage
8 times led league in Doubles
5 times led league in Runs Scored
6 times led league in Total Bases
5 times led league in Triples
7 times led league in Extra-base hits

DiMaggio

3 AL MVPs
2 Batting titles
2 HR titles
2 RBI titles
0 times led league in On-base Percentage
2 times led league in Slugging Percentage
0 times led league in Doubles
1 time led league in Runs Scored
3 times led league in Total Bases
1 time led league in Triples
2 times led league in Extra-base hits

DiMaggio didn't put up the stalwart numbers like Musial and Williams did, however he was an American icon and few athletes can say that. Musial was probably the best all-around hitter of all-time and the most beloved/well-liked figure in the game's history. Williams in his prime was the best. For what he accomplished and could have achieved, Williams might have gone down as the "Best Ever." That statement trumps both his rivals.

My Rankings

1. Ted Williams
2. Joe DiMaggio
3. Stan Musial

5. Mickey Mantle-Willie Mays-Duke Snider

"Willie, Mickey and The Duke." Sing it with me again. "Willie, Mickey, and The Duke." This popular song by singer-songwriter Terry Cashman in the 1950s was a tribute to the three phenomenal baseball players that each patrolled centerfield for the three New York teams -- New York Yankees, Brooklyn Dodgers and New York Giants -- during the sports most stimulating decade that was dubbed "The Golden Age of Baseball." Big Apple fans had nothing but options of who they wanted to watch. They could watch the Giants play in the Polo Grounds in Upper Manhattan; the Yankees play in the Bronx at historic Yankee Stadium or the Dodgers play in Brooklyn at vintage Ebbets Field. It was a baseball fans dream if you were a New Yorker. Willie Mays was the

Giants enthusiastic, blissful, classic five-tool player; Mickey Mantle was the Yankees larger-than-life, astonishing all-around talent and Duke Snider was the Dodgers brilliant, somewhat discounted enforcer. I can only imagine the delight and jubilation of baseball fans in New York during that time. Their excitement level had to be off the rhetoric scale. You had three outstanding, championship-caliber teams all playing in one city led by a trio of players that captivated the city's attention and imagination to the certain stint where all New York fans were fixated on the constant debate of who's better: Mays, Mantle or Snider?

Mays and Mantle were clearly more recognizable than Snider during their playing days but The Duke became a star first. In Snider's first two seasons (1947 and 1948), he didn't make much of an impact; yet 1949 was when he started making his presence known -- batting .244, hitting 23 homeruns, 92 RBIs and helping the Dodgers win the NL pennant, although they fell in the World Series to the Yankees in five games. Snider's numbers would jump in 1950 (batted .321, hit 31 HRs, drove in 107 RBIs) and established himself as the essential go-to hitter in a loaded Dodgers lineup that included future Hall of Famers Jackie Robinson, Roy Campanella, Pee Wee Reese, and all-stars Gil Hodges and Carl Furillo. Mays and Mantle took centerstage for their clubs in 1951 and both struggled early on before adjusting and hitting their stride. Mantle was called up to the majors in April to play rightfield beside Yankees great and soon-to-be retired Joe DiMaggio but after a short slump he was sent back to the minors. Mantle would gain his form back and return to New York to help them reach the World Series. After a 1-for-26 start, the 20-year-old Mays would soon get rolling and would win NL Rookie of the Year. While Mays and Mantle were getting their feet wet in the big leagues, Snider's Dodgers were building a 13-game lead in the National League at season's end. On August 12, Mays' Giants began a 16-game win streak and took 37 of their final 44 games to pull into a first-place tie with the Dodgers. The two would square off in a three-game playoff to decide the NL pennant. Both teams split the first two games and the deciding game was played at the Polo Grounds. In dramatic fashion, with the Dodgers up 4-2 in the ninth inning with runners on second and third and Mays on deck, Giants third baseman Bobby Thomson stepped up to the plate against right-hander Ralph Branca and delivered a three-run homer known as, "The Shot Heard 'Round the World" to win the pennant and complete one of the greatest comebacks in baseball history. Thomson's famous homerun culminated into Giants play-by-play announcer Russ Hodges memorable call of, "The Giants win the pennant, the Giants win the pennant, the Giants win the pennant! I don't believe it, I don't believe it, I don't believe it!" It remains still to this day as one of the greatest moments in baseball history.

The 1951 World Series matchup between the powerful Yankees and the upstart Giants pitted the two future baseball superstars -- Mays and Mantle -- against each other. The Giants put up a fight; however the Bronx Bombers had a little too much pitching -- winning the title in six games. The next year, Mantle (.311 average, 23 HRs, 87 RBIs) would replace DiMaggio in centerfield, reach superstardom in his sophomore season and lead the Yankees back to the World Series, where they defeated Snider's (.303 average, 21 HRs, 92 RBIs) Dodgers in a tightly-matched, well-played Fall Classic 4 games to 3. With Mays playing only 34 games in '52 and missing all of the '53 season due to being drafted into the Army, the Yankees and Dodgers continued to separate themselves from the rest of baseball. In 1953, both teams dominated the competition with the Dodgers going 105-49, winning the NL by a convincing 13 games and the Yankees took the AL by 8 ½ games at 99-52. In a highly anticipated Fall Classic rematch, both teams trotted out loaded, top-to-bottom lineups and between the two teams featured a total of nine Hall of Fame players (Yankees: Mantle, Yogi Berra, Whitey Ford, Johnny Mize, Phil Rizutto; Dodgers: Snider, 1953 NL MVP Roy Campanella, Pee Wee Reese, and Jackie Robinson), and you can also include Yankees Hall of Fame manager Casey Stengel in the mix. This might have been the most overall talent ever in a World Series and all of New York had front row seats to the action. The teams split the first four games but The Mick broke the series open by hitting a grand slam to win game 5 and the Yankees closed the series out in game 6 at home 4-3 to clinch an all-time record, probably never to be duplicated again fifth consecutive World Series title. Snider batted .320, hit 1 homer, and had 5 RBIs for the series, given Mantle was a notch better, batting only .208, but produced 2 homers and 7 RBIs for the series. It was unfortunate for the city of Brooklyn because the '53 Dodgers turned out to be one of the best baseball squads never to win it all. They just couldn't overcome the force of the Yankees Empire. What can I say; New York had Brooklyn's number.

The centerfield competition only thickened as Mays returned for his first full season in 1954 and boy, it was enduring. The 1954 season marked the first time in Mays career he was thrusted into the limelight. Mantle had his strongest season up to that point (.300 average, 27 HRs, 102 RBIs), however the Yankees run of five straight titles came to an end by the 111-win Cleveland Indians (an American League record for wins that stood for 44 years). The Giants and Dodgers were at it again scrapping it out for the NL pennant. Snider (.341 average, 40

HRs, 130 RBIs) boasted a MVP-type season, although Mays (.345 average, 41 HRs, 110 RBIs) outdueled Snider, winning the NL MVP and lifted his Giants past the Dodgers in the standings by 5 games for the pennant. The 1954 World Series belonged to the Giants after upsetting the heavy-favored Indians in a sweep and the series would best be remembered for "The Catch", a sensational, over-the-shoulder catch by Mays that prevented a go-ahead run for the Indians in the eighth inning of game 1. That was Mays' first and only title. In 1955, Mantle's Yankees and Snider's Dodgers would do battle in another Fall Classic. After a number of near-misses to the Yankees (1947, 1949, 1952, 1953), the Dodgers finally triumphed past the Yankees in seven games, bringing natural joy to Brooklyn -- at least for one year. The Yankees restored order in '56 defeating the Dodgers in seven, in what was their last Subway Series matchup. Mantle not only walked away with his fourth ring in '56, but he also put together one of the greatest individual seasons of all-time, winning the Triple Crown (.353 average, 52 HRs, 130 RBIs) and the AL MVP. As Mantle did his thing in '56, Mays hit 36 homers and stole 40 bases, becoming the second player ever to reach the "30-30 club" (30 HRs and 30 stolen bases in the same season), and Snider had a heck of a year himself hitting 43 HRs and 101 RBIs. This debate continued to steam.

Going into the 1957 season, the only baseball teams that seemed to matter were the Yankees, Dodgers and Giants and in all actuality -- they were. That would change when the Yankees fell to the up-and-coming, young Milwaukee Braves and NL MVP Hank Aaron in the World Series. That didn't stop the NY trio from performing though. Mantle won his second straight AL MVP award (batting .333, hitting 34 homers, 94 RBIs), and led the league in runs scored and walks. Mays (batted .333, hit 35 homers, drove in 97 RBIs, stole 38 bases) became the fourth player in history to join the "20-20-20 club" (doubles, triples, homeruns) and became the second player ever to have 20 homers, 20 doubles, 20 triples, and 20 steals in the same season. Snider punched in 40 homers and 92 RBIs. 1957 was the last season all three would play centerfield in the same city. The Dodgers and Giants shockingly moved to California -- the Dodgers to Los Angeles and the Giants to San Francisco. The triumvirate broke up but they still continued their success, only this time in different regions of the U.S. Snider helped lead the Dodgers to their first title in L.A. in 1959, Mays sustained his brilliant all-around play for another decade and Mantle (whose Yankees defeated Mays' Giants in the 1962 World Series), would win three more championships and continue asserting himself as one of the all-time great Yankees besides the likes of Ruth, Gehrig and DiMaggio.

Boy I would love to have a picture and autograph of these three.

There's only one bat to go around fellas!

Mick and Willie sharing the bat.

Mantle smacking one deep.

Three Hall of Famers sharing some old memories in 1995.

So, Who's Better- Though the "Willie, Mickey, and The Duke" debate was fun in New York during the '50s, let's try to settle the score once and for all. Many thought there was a strong gap between Mays and Mantle from Snider, but looking at the season averages of all three players during their respected primes from 1954-1957, the stats suggest otherwise:

Mays- .323 batting average, 41 HRs, 104 RBIs, 114 runs, 28 stolen bases

Mantle- .330 batting average, 38 HRs, 106 RBIs, 126 runs, 10 stolen bases

Snider- .305 batting average, 41 HRs, 115 RBIs, 112 runs, 5 stolen bases

Snider's stats were right on par or slightly better than his crosstown rivals. Does it make him equal or better than Willie and Mickey? Absolutely not. This is a whole career we're talking about -- not just four years. Snider was a Hall of Famer and a smashing player, still he's not on the level of Mays and Mantle. He didn't have the speed or power and wasn't the terrific athlete his two rivals were. Mantle was maybe as gifted as any baseball player ever. He was a 3-time MVP. As a switch-hitter, he hit the ball probably longer than anyone. He was the best player on those powerhouse Yankee squads during the '50s and early '60s that won 12 AL pennants and 7 World Series titles. He was one of the best postseason performers ever -- he holds the record for the most World Series homeruns (18), RBIs (40), runs (42), extra-base hits (26), walks (43) and total bases (123). The Mick could do it all, although injuries during his career limited his defense and base running. His excessive drinking and partying also contributed to his production sliding and body breaking down. Mantle was one of the all-time greats and many believe he could have been better than what he actually was, if not for the injuries and fraternizing but Mays was just better.

To me, Mays was the most complete player ever and the greatest defensive outfielder of all-time. No player could beat you in more ways than Mays. He was the true essence of a five-tool player. He could hit for power, hit for average, field, run and throw. He won 2 NL MVP awards (probably should have won more), won a record-tying 12 Gold Glove awards, made a record-tying 24 All-Star Games, is a member of the 3,000-hit club (Mantle and Snider can't say that), hit 660 homeruns (4th all-time), batted .302 for his career (Mantle and Snider batted below .300 for their career), led the NL in stolen bases 4 times, and was the first player to hit 300 HRs and steal 300 bases. Mays was a versatile beast and that's why he wins this historic debate. Here that, Say Hey Kid, YOU WIN! You can show off your boyish smile now!

My Rankings

1. **Willie Mays**
2. **Mickey Mantle**
3. **Duke Snider**

4. Bjorn Borg-Jimmy Connors-John McEnroe

You had a Swedish righty and two American lefties battling for tennis royalty in the mid-1970s through the mid-1980s entitled, "The Golden Age of Tennis" and largely responsible for the sport flourishing in America. Sorry Ivan Lendl, if this was a rivalry stretching out to a foursome, then you would have definitely been included but you didn't become a formidable threat on the tour until 1981-1982 -- when Borg was on his way out and McEnroe/Connors were the top two players in the game. Bjorn Borg was a cool, calm customer on the court that never seemed rattled (nicknamed "Ice") who played a peculiar style. Borg played from the baseline, utilizing a rare two-hand backhand, hit his shots with substantial topspin, had powerful ground strokes, used a serve-and-volley tactic, mixed it up with a chipping approach, and was known for being the best physically, conditioned player during his playing days. Jimmy Connors can best be described as the Energizer Bunny. Surprisingly taught the game by his mother and grandmother, Connors (nicknamed "Jimbo") was audacious and fiery on the court, with his behavior being sometimes crude and shocking to tennis fans, who were used to seeing tennis players with better mannerisms. He never gave in to his opponents or showed vulnerability and was notorious for always getting the crowd pumped and out of their seats; cheering him on to give him an extra boast. Connors wasn't as big and didn't hit the ball with the power and speed as his competitors did but his grit and determination stood out more than anything. His main weapon was his unique, yet corky two-hand backhand that he hit flat and low and his efficient, more-than-capable serve. John McEnroe was the ultimate serve-and-volleyer of his time, possessing tremendous footwork, quickness, slicing tactics, and shotmaking ability. McEnroe had a unique serve, serving with his back turned almost fully to his opponent -- mixing his serve up with speed, precision, spin and good placement to fool and many times jam the opposition. Nicknamed "Fire", McEnroe was best known for his outrageous, ill-tempered on-court behavior towards tennis umpires that often resulted in him belittling officials in a demonstrative manner.

After having a successful college career at UCLA, winning the NCAA singles title as a freshman in 1971, Connors turned pro the next year and started out with a bang. He won six titles in 1972 and eleven in 1973, to finish the year ranked third. Then in 1974, Connors would conquer over tennis, producing one of the premier seasons the game has ever seen: going 99-4, winning 15 tournaments, won three Slams (Australian Open, Wimbledon, U.S. Open), just missing out on achieving the Calendar Year Grand Slam and finished the year at No.1.

(Connors was banned from playing in the 1974 French Open because he signed a contract to play (WTT) World Team Tennis and the French Tennis Federation didn't allow WTT players to play because it conflicted with the French Open. Connors could not play in the French Open until 1979 because from 1974 to 1978, all WTT players could not play in the tournament). What a pity too, because the way Connors was playing in '74, he probably would have won in Paris. Would we have looked at Connors' career in a different perspective if he would have achieved the Calendar Year Grand Slam? Probably so. It's a classic "What If" example.

Pop Question: Who do you think took advantage of Connors absence at the French Open in '74? That would be Bjorn Rune Borg. Borg was in his second year as a pro at the time, the youngest ever French Open winner at the bare age of 18. He would retain his French title in 1975 defeating lofty, clay-courter Guillermo Villas in straight sets (6-2, 6-3, 6-4). As Borg continued to move up the ladder and stake his claim as one of the best players in the world, Connors maintained his place as the top player in the men's game in 1975 -- punching in nine titles but surprisingly no Grand Slam titles, finishing runner-up in the same three Slams he won the previous year. In 1976, Borg fell short of three-peating at the French Open, losing in the quarterfinals (which would be the last match he ever lost on the clay courts in Paris), yet found gratitude in becoming the youngest Wimbledon champion at the age of 20, until Boris Becker won Wimbledon at 17 in 1985. Meanwhile, the No.1 player Connors was winless in the last four grand slams he entered but he got back on the right track taking the 1976 U.S. Open title by defeating Borg (6-4, 3-6, 7-6, 6-4 on clay courts that year) in their first Grand Slam final against each other. The rivalry was about to heat up going into 1977: Enter John McEnroe to join the fun! As an 18-year-old amateur, McEnroe would make it through the qualifying tournament and into the main draw of Wimbledon in 1977, where he became the youngest player and first qualifier to reach the semifinals at a Grand Slam tournament, only to lose to his future American rival, Connors in four sets (6-3, 6-3, 4-6, 6-4). The '77 Wimbledon Final featured the top two seeds, Borg and Connors against each other, with Borg winning an exceptional five-setter (3-6, 6-2, 6-1, 5-7, 6-4). Winning back-to-back Wimbledon crowns lifted Borg up to the top world ranking but only for a week before Connors seized back the top spot. At the Grand Prix year-end championships in New York, Connors would get a little revenge on Borg, winning the title and eventually finishing the year at No. 1 again.

In 1978, with the young McEnroe struggling to find his game, Borg was starting to hit the peak of his career. Borg became the second player in the Open era (Rod Laver was the first) to complete the infrequent accomplishment of winning the French-Wimbledon summer double (winning both majors in the same summer, on two completely different surfaces -- clay and grass -- and only a few weeks apart from each other). In a Wimbledon final rematch, Borg took it to Connors (6-4, 6-2, 6-2) to lay claim to his third straight All-England Club trophy. Borg's confidence was riding sky high going into the 1978 U.S. Open (first U.S. Open on hard courts), while Connors was looking for answers after losing his last three grand slam finals, two of them to Borg. The top two men on the planet met in the U.S. Open final, where Connors found his answers defeating Borg in a take charge effort (6-4, 6-2, 6-2). It was Connors third U.S. Open win and remains the only player in history to win the U.S. Open on three different surfaces -- grass, clay and hard courts. The 1979 season served as Borg's finest: producing an 84-6 record, won 13 titles, both French and Wimbledon titles, and for most of the year was ranked No. 1. By winning his first Grand Slam title at the 1979 U.S. Open (beating Connors along the way in the semifinals), the blossoming McEnroe was making the jump to the top and making his presence known to the rest of the tennis globe.

At this point in Connors' career, entering the 1980 season, he was still an elite player that was capable of winning grand slams but for the time being had to settle for being "third best" behind Borg and Johnny Mac. If McEnroe was the Prince of Tennis, then Borg was The King. In order to reach Borg's throne, McEnroe knew he would have to inch closer to overtaking his crown. After winning at Roland Garros for the fifth time, Borg marched into Wimbledon as the clear favorite seeking his fifth straight title. McEnroe as the No. 2 seed and Connors as the No. 3 seed battled in the semifinals, with McEnroe winning (6-3, 3-6, 6-3, 6-4) to advance to the final to meet the No. 1 seed and four-time champ. The final turned out to be unforgettable. McEnroe sliced through Borg in the first set 6-1. Borg took the next two sets 7-5, 6-3. Trailing 5-4 and facing two championship points in the fourth set, McEnroe held off Borg just enough to send the match into a tiebreak. In the tiebreaker, McEnroe saved an unbelievable five match points and six set points to win the set 7-6 (18-16). As the pressure mounted for both players in the fifth set, their games rose to the level that was needed to lift the trophy. Borg's serve picked up, at one point winning 19 straight points off his serve in the final set to prevail 8-6. It was Borg's fifth straight Wimbledon title and third year in a row he completed the French-Wimbledon double. The 1980 Wimbledon final between Borg and McEnroe will live in tennis fans minds forever and is considered today as the greatest tennis match of all-time, alongside the 2008 Wimbledon men's final between the #1 and #2 players at the time, Roger Federer and Rafael Nadal. After the final, the tennis nation was anticipating a Borg-McEnroe rematch and fans wouldn't have to wait long. After McEnroe defeated Connors in the 1980 U.S. Open semifinal in an intriguing contest (6-4, 5-7, 0-6, 6-3, 7-6), the rematch was on in the final. Playing on hard courts (McEnroe's best surface), he would exact his revenge, beating Borg in a classic match (7-6, 6-1, 6-7, 5-7, 6-4). The McEnroe-Borg saga would continue in 1981. Borg won his record sixth French Open title, beating up-and-coming Ivan Lendl in the final and next up was Wimbledon.

Borg was still the pick to win in London (barely), however Johnny Mac was lurking. In order to reach the final, Borg found himself in a real dogfight with Connors in the semifinals, who for the last year-and-a-half was being overshadowed by all the hype surrounding McEnroe and Borg. Connors came out like gangbusters taking the first two sets but Borg would stage a comeback, coming from behind to win (0-6, 4-6, 6-3, 6-0, 6-4) and meet McEnroe for the much-awaited Wimbledon sequel. Borg entered the final with a Wimbledon record 41-match winning streak (still stands today), that McEnroe would break, winning his first Wimbledon title in triumphant fashion (4-6, 7-6, 7-6, 6-4). The U.S. Open would play out the same way. Borg defeated Connors in the semifinals and McEnroe defeated Borg in the final in four sets. McEnroe became the first male player to win three consecutive U.S. Open titles since Bill Tilden won six straight in the 1920s, and most importantly ended the year at No. 1. For Borg, it would be the last Grand Slam event he would play. Borg would only play one tournament in 1982 and in January 1983, he shockingly retired at the tender age of 26 -- still in the prime of his career. Nobody was more disappointed than McEnroe himself. His biggest rival and competition was gone. He tried several times to reach out to Borg to convince him to return to the game and renew their rivalry but he was unsuccessful. With Borg gone, the door opened up for Connors in 1982 to move to the forefront of men's tennis with McEnroe and he did just that. The Bad Boys of Tennis were now the two best players in the game and would get a chance to tangle against one another in their first Grand Slam final at Wimbledon in '82. Connors was down two sets to one and in a fourth-set tiebreaker, McEnroe was three points from the title, though Connors rallied to win the fourth set and later the match (3-6, 6-3, 6-7, 7-6, 6-4) for his first Grand Slam title in four years. 1982 proved to be a season of resurgence for Connors, who also won the U.S. Open that year.

During the 1982 and 1983 seasons, McEnroe and Connors flip-flopped the No. 1 ranking a crazy eleven different times. Talk about a back-and-forth encounter! You can say the two were in a good old American War and neither was laying down their guns to surrender. McEnroe jumped ahead of his nemesis and the rest of the field in 1984, putting together perhaps the greatest season in men's tennis history. Johnny Mac compiled a fantastic 82-3 record (96.5% winning percentage), won 13 tournaments and took home 2 Slams. Following probably the toughest loss of his career, losing the '84 French Open final to Ivan Lendl after being up two sets to zero, McEnroe went on to annihilate Connors in the Wimbledon final (6-1, 6-1, 6-2) and capture his fourth U.S. Open title by defeating Lendl in the final, who at the time was evolving as the men's top player. To make 1984 even sweeter for McEnroe, he defeated Connors at all three Slams -- semifinals at the French Open, finals at Wimbledon and the semifinals of the U.S. Open. (Outside of the Australian Open for whatever reason the major players never played in the event until the mid-to-late 1980s). As the decade went on, Connors and McEnroe continued competing but neither would reach top form again -- with a budding new generation of players such as Lendl, Mats Wilander, Pat Cash, Boris Becker and Stefan Edberg set to take over the men's game.

Here are some absorbing numbers and facts about the three that set them apart from the rest of the competition:

- The men's year-end No. 1 rankings from 1974 to 1984:

    1974- Jimmy Connors
    1975- Jimmy Connors
    1976- Jimmy Connors
    1977- Jimmy Connors
    1978- Jimmy Connors
    1979- Bjorn Borg
    1980- Bjorn Borg
    1981- John McEnroe
    1982- John McEnroe
    1983- John McEnroe
    1984- John McEnroe

- From 1974-1984, one of the three players won at least one Grand Slam title every year.

- In a stretch from the 1978 Australian Open to the 1981 U.S. Open, when Borg, Connors and McEnroe were all on the tour at the same time, the three combined to win 12 Grand Slam titles out of 16 Grand Slam Tournaments (Borg 7, McEnroe 4, Connors 1).

- ATP Player of the Year award winners from 1976-1984:

1976- Bjorn Borg	1981- John McEnroe
1977- Bjorn Borg	1982- Jimmy Connors
1978- Bjorn Borg	1983- John McEnroe
1979- Bjorn Borg	1984- John McEnroe
1980- Bjorn Borg	

- In nine straight Grand Slam tournaments from the 1979 Wimbledon to the 1981 Wimbledon, seven times Connors, Borg, and McEnroe were seeded 1-2-3 in the tournaments, in some order.

- From 1976-1984, either Borg, McEnroe, or Connors won Wimbledon (Borg 5, McEnroe 3, Connors 1).

- From 1978-1984, either McEnroe or Connors won the U.S. Open (McEnroe 4, Connors 3).

This is pretty much saying from the mid-1970s to the mid-1980s, the Borg-Connors-McEnroe troika ruled men's tennis!

The No. 1 (Borg) and No. 2 (McEnroe) players in the world right before their treasured 1980 Wimbledon Final.

The two rivals chasing the ball down on the grass courts of Wimbledon.

The Bad Boys of Tennis.

Borg and Connors walking on to Centre Court for the 1977 Wimbledon Final.

The 1974 Australian Open Champion, Jimmy Connors.

Johnny Mac kissing the U.S. Open trophy in 1984.

A typical site after Wimbledon: Borg lifting the All England Club Cup.

So, Who's Better- There is no clear-cut answer for this decision. Translation: All three can make a strong case for being the best out of this group.

Let's first take a look at the all-time head-to-head records versus one another:

<u>Bjorn Borg</u>
15-8 vs. **Connors**
4-2 vs. Connors in Grand Slam matches
2-2 vs. Connors in Grand Slam Finals

7-7 vs. **McEnroe**
1-3 vs. McEnroe in Grand Slam matches
1-3 vs. McEnroe in Grand Slam Finals

-22-15 combined record

<u>Jimmy Connors</u>
8-15 vs. **Borg**
2-4 vs. Borg in Grand Slam matches
2-2 vs. Borg in Grand Slam Finals

14-20 vs. **McEnroe**
3-6 vs. McEnroe in Grand Slam matches
1-1 vs. McEnroe in Grand Slam Finals

-22-35 combined record

<u>John McEnroe</u>
7-7 vs. **Borg**
3-1 vs. Borg in Grand Slam matches
3-1 vs. Borg in Grand Slam Finals

20-14 vs. **Connors**
6-3 vs. Connors in Grand Slam matches
1-1 vs. Connors in Grand Slam Finals

-27-21 combined record

They're three of the top 10 men's tennis players ever. That's for sure. None of them achieved the Career Grand Slam (winning all four majors in your career) but all three had brilliant careers. Borg won 11 Grand

Slam titles (T-4th all-time), Connors won 8 (T-6th all-time) and McEnroe won 7 (T-7th all-time); although, as you can see, Connors had a losing record against both McEnroe and Borg overall and in Grand Slam matches. The thing is for most of Connors' career, he battled his two counterparts when they were three or four years younger than him. You can say they had fresher legs in their matches together than Connors did. He was like the elder statesman on the tour compared to the two. Knowing that, you still have to take in consideration that Connors was still in his prime and very daunting when he battled Johnny Mac and Borg during those golden years of tennis, and really…they just had Jimbo's number. Connors had his moments against his two rivals, yet in comprehensive -- they got the best of him. He might not be able to win this argument but he surely had the better career of the three. (You also can't forget the fact that Connors played longer and better late in his career than Borg and McEnroe. Strong example: His cherished run to the U.S. Open semifinals in 1991 at the elderly age of 39). Neither Borg nor McEnroe won three Slams in one year like Connors did in 1974. Connors has won the most singles titles (109) in men's tennis history (McEnroe has 77 and Borg 63) and is the only male player with 100 or more singles titles. Connors has the most match wins (1,242) of all-time and has been ranked No. 1 for more weeks (268) than McEnroe (170) and Borg (109). He was the No. 1 ranked player in the world for a record 160 consecutive weeks, until Roger Federer broke the record staying at No. 1 for 237 consecutive weeks. A pretty awesome resume for Connors, although Borg and McEnroe will battle for the top spot.

McEnroe was No. 1 for more weeks and won more singles titles than Borg but most importantly Borg has 11 Slams to Johnny Mac's 7. Debate over, right? Hold on, now. Yes, Borg captured more Slams but he was 1-3 versus McEnroe in Grand Slam finals and many media members believe he drove Borg out of the game because he started to crawl into his head (the whole mental psyche thing) and Borg's confidence started to wane after losing three straight Slam finals to McEnroe. (BTW: They faced off at Wimbledon and the U.S. Open but never at the French Open. It's a pity because it only would have added another element to their already incredible rivalry and would have been great cinema. Borg probably would have had McEnroe's number at Roland Garros though. He was insanely good on clay. More on that in a few). We still don't know for sure why Borg walked away from tennis early, though I get the feeling from watching the HBO documentary: *McEnroe/Borg: Fire & Ice*, that it had something to do with McEnroe leapfrogging Borg as the best player in the world and he just couldn't handle not being No. 1 anymore. We might never know, but if that's true, then it has to count for something, right? It's a difficult choice, nonetheless here's where Borg might have a sparse lead over McEnroe in my mind. Borg was a masterful clay and grass court player, winning six French Open titles (second all-time after Rafael Nadal in the Open Era) and five Wimbledon titles (he won Wimbledon five consecutive times). Not only did he win the French Open and Wimbledon multiple times but he dominated those events. He *owned* them. Borg owned the French Open and Wimbledon the same way Jordan and Russell owned the NBA Finals, the way Montana owned the Super Bowl, the way the Yankees owned the World Series, the way Gretzky and Wilt owned scoring records, the way Oscar and Magic owned the triple-double, the way Nicklaus owned The Masters, the way Navratilova and Sampras owned Wimbledon, the way Evert owned the French Open, the way Jesse Owens owned the 1936 Olympics, the way Ali and Louis owned the boxing ring, the way Pele owned the soccer pitch and the way Ruth defined the homerun. You get the point. Borg made these tournaments something of his own. It was his and his alone. McEnroe won the U.S. Open four times and Connors won the U.S. Open five times but you can never say that they *owned* that event, much less, any other Slam. They didn't put or leave an imprint on the U.S. Open the way Borg did at Paris and London.

For the greats, it's all about how many Slams/majors you win. Borg won eleven, plus he was a very good hard court player, finishing as a four-time finalist at the U.S. Open (a three-time runner-up when the event was played on hard courts). If he would have won at least one U.S. Open title, then he would have solidified this debate. Borg dominated men's tennis more, had more consistent seasons (he's tied for the most consecutive years (eight) for winning at least one Slam title) and most vitally, he won more Grand Slams than Connors and McEnroe did. That's just enough to push him over the edge.

My Rankings

1. Bjorn Borg
2. John McEnroe
3. Jimmy Connors

3. Joe Montana-Dan Marino-John Elway

Maybe my favorite three-way rivalry on the list. Arguably three of the five greatest quarterbacks in NFL history. Without a question the three best quarterbacks of the 1980s and early 1990s. One was as cool, calm, instinctive and accurate as any quarterback ever; the other known for his quick release, exceptional pocket presence and lofty passing numbers; and the other a true, gritty competitor who had sublime scrambling and playmaking ability, and excelled repeatedly in late game situations. The troika of John Elway, Dan Marino and Joe Montana came along at a time when NFL offenses were starting to shift from "establishing the running game first and controlling the line of scrimmage" to "a bigger emphasis on passing the football more and dominating the game through the air, by using a multitude of offensive plays to throw short, long, horizontally and vertically." Montana, Elway and Marino each embodied the evolution of the "drop back, pass-happy, spread the ball all over the field, I'm going to put constant pressure on the defense, and control and dictate the outcome of the game" type quarterback. What made this rivalry so high on the list was the power struggle between the three signal-callers for the title belt of "Best QB on the Planet" during the '80s. It's not that the three quarterbacks got caught up in the stiff competition against each other, but it was more of the fans and media creating the buzz and building this rivalry up to becoming a fascinating sports debate. And it was.

Check out a few of the major quarterback statistics all-time for the three Hall of Famers:

<u>Most Passing Yards in NFL History</u>
2. Dan Marino- 61,361
4. John Elway- 51,475
12. Joe Montana- 40,551

<u>Most Touchdown Passes in NFL History</u>
2. Dan Marino- 420
5. John Elway- 300
11. Joe Montana- 273

<u>Most Completions in NFL History</u>
2. Dan Marino- 4,967
4. John Elway- 4,123
11. Joe Montana- 3,409

<u>Most Passing Attempts in NFL History</u>
2. Dan Marino- 8,358
3. John Elway- 7,250
12. Joe Montana- 5,391

<u>Most Wins by a Quarterback in NFL History</u>
2. John Elway- 148
3. Dan Marino- 147
8. Joe Montana- 117

The three are standing pretty tall with numbers like that. Marino and Elway finished in the top two in all five categories but Montana finished with a higher career completion percentage (63.2%) to Marino's (59.4%) and Elway's (56.9%), a higher career winning percentage (.713%) to Elway's (.643%) and Marino's (.613%), and a higher career passer rating (92.3) to Marino's (86.4) and Elway's (79.9). Does Marino and Elway's bulky career numbers put them above Montana historically? Can't tell the audience that until my 'So, Who's Better' section. Be patient now!

Joe Montana was the first of the three quarterbacks to get their professional football career formed. Coming out of Notre Dame, where he led the Fighting Irish to a National Championship in his junior year, Montana was known for his improbable comebacks, most notably in the 1979 Cotton Bowl against Houston. With Montana dealing with hypothermia and the flu on an icy day and Notre Dame trailing 34-12 after three quarters, he rallied the troops to a dramatic comeback victory 35-34 in one of the best college football acts in history. Despite his firm performances in college, Montana was only a third-round pick in the 1979 NFL Draft by San Francisco. Montana served as the 49ers backup the majority of his rookie season but became the starter midway through the 1980 season, which the 49ers finished 6-10. In 1981, the 49ers enjoyed a complete turnaround, posting a NFL-best 13-3 record, under Montana mastering head coach Bill Walsh's West Coast offense that was predicated on timing, rhythm, motion and short passes. The offense turned out to be tailor-made for Montana. San Francisco snuck past Dallas in the NFC title game, behind Montana famously throwing a game-winning six-yard touchdown pass to wide receiver Dallas Clark in the back of the end zone with 51 seconds left, recognized as "The Catch." In the Big Game against the Cincinnati Bengals, Montana threw for 157 yards, one touchdown pass, and had one rushing touchdown to take Super Bowl MVP honors and lead the 49ers to victory 26-21. Because of a player's strike that lasted 57 days, the 1982 season was reduced from 16 games to nine. The 49ers missed the playoffs at 3-6 but Montana did play well, throwing for 2,163 yards and 17 touchdowns. Going into the 1983 season, highly-touted rookie quarterbacks -- John Elway from Stanford (Denver Broncos) and Dan Marino out of Pittsburgh (Miami Dolphins) -- would join Montana in the league.

From 1983 to 1991, the three simultaneously would be at the forefront of the NFL, carrying their respective teams and playing the quarterback position at a marvelously, skyscraping level. Let's chronicle every season from 1983-1991 for each player:

1983: Elway's rookie campaign was at best up-and-down, while Marino's turned out to be one of the best ever by a rookie quarterback. Elway struggled, throwing 14 interceptions to 7 touchdown passes but managed to get the 9-7 Broncos to the playoffs -- only to get smoked by the Seattle Seahawks 31-7 in the Wild Card game. Down in Miami, Marino put together the finest year of any rookie quarterback up to that point, throwing 20 touchdown passes in 11 games, won Rookie of the Year, became the first rookie to lead their conference in passer rating (96.0) since the 1970 AFL-NFL merger and was the first rookie to start in the Pro Bowl. Freakin ridiculous! That ain't all either. He led the Dolphins to a 12-4 record (tied for the AFC-best with the Oakland Raiders), although the Dolphins got upset at home by the same Seahawks that sent Elway's Broncos home in the previous round. This was not the last time the rest of the league would here from Marino. Montana, on the other end, had a Pro Bowl type season himself, throwing for 3,910 yards, 26 touchdown passes to 12 interceptions. He led the 49ers to a 10-6 record, past the Detroit Lions in a close affair 24-23 in the divisional round, where Montana threw a go-ahead touchdown pass with 1:23 left in the game. In the NFC title game versus the defending Super Bowl champion Washington Redskins, the 49ers trailed 21-0 heading into the fourth quarter, though Montana led them back, tossing three scores to even the game at 21-21. That is until, Redskins kicker, 1982 NFL MVP Mark Moseley (Laugh if you want. I'm not joking. A kicker really won the MVP award that season!) kicked the go-ahead field goal with 40 seconds left to win 24-21.

ADVANTAGE: Yes, Marino's rookie season was no joke and showed he would be a force for years to come but Montana at this point was more established, had the better overall year, and got his team one win away from the Big Game. **MONTANA** gets the nod.

1984: What stood out this season was Montana, Marino and Elway -- in that order -- led their teams to a 1-2-3 finish for the top three records in football. Go figure! Elway improved from his first season, bumping up to 18 touchdown passes, even though his interceptions was still up at 15; nonetheless, he led the Broncos to the #2 seed in the AFC at 13-3 behind the league's No. 2 defense. Remember when I said after Marino's rookie season that it would not be the last time the league would hear from him? Well, the league sure as hell heard from him in 1984! Marino's 48 TD passes was an NFL record that stood for 20 years. His record 5,084 passing yards that season stood for 27 years until Drew Brees (5,476) and Tom Brady (5,235) broke the mark in 2011. He led the league in completions, attempts, passing yards per game, passer rating, won the NFL MVP, was the NFL Offensive Player of the Year and was a First Team All-Pro. What can you say; Marino was All-World in '84. The man produced the greatest quarterback season ever to that point. What made the season even better was putting the Dolphins in title contention with a 14-2 record and the #1 seed in the AFC. Montana in '84 was at the peak of his powers. He was a Second Team All-Pro, threw for 3,360 yards, 28 TD passes, 10 INTs, carried the 49ers to an NFL-best 15-1 record and was the big favorites to win the whole thang heading into the playoffs. What looked like a possible AFC Championship Game matchup between Marino's Dolphins and Elway's Broncos fell short, with the Broncos getting upset by the Pittsburgh Steelers 24-17. The Dolphins and their explosive attack cruised past Seattle 31-10 and lit up Pittsburgh 45-28 in the AFC title game, led by Marino's 421 passing yards-4 TD pass-1 INT performance. Meanwhile the 49ers looked strong as ever in the NFC. Montana tossed up 309 yards and 3 TD passes in a divisional playoff win against the New York Giants 21-10, then the league's No. 1 defense put the clamps down on the Chicago Bears 23-0 in the NFC title game. The showdown for Super Bowl XIX was set.

The game featured the two best teams in the league, the two best offenses (Dolphins at No.1, 49ers at No.2) and the top two quarterbacks in football. Super Bowl XIX turned out to be one of the most highly anticipated games in sports history and the central reason was because of all the excitement surrounding the Montana-Marino QB matchup. Marino was the "hot new thing" and the chatter by the media during the weeks leading up to the game was that Marino had surpassed Montana as the best at their position. The game was expected to be an offensive shootout and had the makings of a timeless championship game. The Dolphins started nicely, taking a 10-7 lead after the first quarter. From there on, the 49ers took charge, winning the game 38-16 behind an outstanding effort from the D and a precise, balanced attack on offense, led by Montana's Super Bowl MVP game -- 24 of 35 passes completed, 331 passing yards, 3 TD passes, 0 INTs, and added 59 rushing yards and 1 rushing TD. Marino finished with 29 completions out of 50, 318 passing yards, 1 TD pass, and was deeply disrupted by the 49ers defense, picking him off twice and sacking him four times. It would surprisingly be Marino's first and only Super Bowl appearance of his career. Montana capped off the season leading the 49ers to an astonishing 18-1 record, a second Super Bowl title and retained his belt as the "Best Quarterback Alive."

ADVANTAGE: I'm tempting to go with a tie between Marino and Montana. Yup, it's that close folks. Marino had a record breaking season. Montana had his best season to that point. Marino was First Team All-Pro. Montana was Second Team All-Pro. Marino was the league MVP. Montana lifted his team to the league's best record. Both players were in the Super Bowl and only one of them won that game...and that was Joe Cool. **MONTANA** in a close one.

1985: Montana and the Super Bowl champion 49ers were primed for another run at the title in '85, until there was this memorable team from Chicago that season (you might have heard of them) that not only interfered with San Francisco's chances of repeating (49ers lost on the road to the Giants in the Wild Card game) but blocked the whole league's chances of sniffing the title. Montana had another first-class season: 3,653 passing yards, 27 TD passes, 13 INTs and led the league in completion percentage. In Denver, Mr. Elway was getting better and improving as an NFL passer. The downside was he threw 23 picks. The bright side was his 22 TD passes and his league-second 3,891 passing yards. The Broncos had another very good year, winning 11 games, although they failed to make the playoffs. Miami, on the other hand, finished 12-4, tied for the AFC-best mark, and were in the running for another Super Bowl appearance. Dan the Man was on fire in '84 and he kept the train rolling in '85, throwing for a league high 4,137 yards, 30 touchdowns and made another First Team All-Pro. Miami advanced to the AFC Championship Game and were favorites to get past the underdog New England Patriots. It would get ugly for Miami. They committed six turnovers and were upset 31-14 at home. I can't understand how Miami couldn't handle that pedestrian Patriots team. They should have been squaring off against the vaulted Bears. Even though Miami came up short of making another Super Bowl appearance, the highlight of their season was by far defeating that mythical '85 Bears team on Monday Night Football -- the Bears only loss that year. (Just for talk, What if we would have gotten that Chicago-Miami rematch that everyone craved for? The one weakness the '85 Bears legendary 46 Defense had that no one seems to mention was their pass defense. They were vulnerable against an elite passing team and it showed when Marino & Co. threw all over them on that Monday Night in December. Was it a strong possibility that Miami could have stolen the luster away from Chicago's season if they would have met in New Orleans? You're damn right they could have. Just saying.)

ADVANTAGE: Elway showed great strides that season and Montana punched in another strong season but Marino was off the charts again and outperformed his counterparts. Also, he was First Team All-Pro for the second straight season. I can't help but to think Marino and the Dolphins blew a wonderful opportunity at getting back to the Big Game and winning it. Oh well. **MARINO** takes this one.

1986: Okay Mr. Elway, I see you. It looks like you have arrived! Elway took his game up a notch in '86. Denver started the season 8-1 and finished 11-5, behind Elway's cannon arm, agile legs and unbelievable playmaking dexterity. He made the Pro Bowl for the first time, by throwing for 3,485 yards and 19 TD passes to 13 INTs. Not eye-popping but highly effective. In the season opener at Tampa Bay, Montana suffered a severe injury to his spinal disc in his lower back that was career-threatening. He was placed on injury reserve but he recovered to return in Week 10, throwing for 270 yards and 3 TD passes in a win vs. the St. Louis Cardinals. Even though he only played in eight games, Montana was able to lead San Francisco to a 10-5-1 record and the NFC West title. It all went up in smoke in the Divisional Playoff game vs. the eventual champion New York Giants, where Montana got knocked out of the game in the second quarter and San Francisco received a nasty beatdown 49-3. It was the only year Montana threw more interceptions (9) than touchdown passes (8). The Dolphins took a step back from the success of the last two seasons by finishing 8-8 and missing the playoffs. If you think that stopped Marino from having another sensational season, then think again! His 4,746 passing yards, 44 TD passes, 378 completions, and 623 attempts were all first in the league and he added to that line by making his third consecutive First Team All-Pro. Meanwhile in the playoffs, Elway introduced to everyone just how clutch he can be. In the AFC Championship Game on the road against the Cleveland Browns, with Denver trailing 20-13 with 5 minutes and 32 seconds to play in the fourth quarter, Elway led his team 98 yards down the field to score the tying touchdown (famously called "The Drive") and sent the game in overtime. Denver won in OT, off a field goal to advance to the Big One. In Super Bowl XXI versus the Giants, Elway played well putting up 304 passing yards, 1 TD pass, 1 rushing TD and threw 1 INT. Behind Giants quarterback Phil Simms stellar MVP outing, and 1986 NFL MVP and Defensive Player of the Year Lawrence Taylor patrolling the Giants menacing defense, they proved to be too much for the Broncos, taking the game 39-20. It was a tough loss for the Broncos but the presumption was Elway would be back in this position many times in the future.

ADVANTAGE: This comes down to Elway and Marino. At this point in his career, Marino was pretty much setting the bar for how productive a quarterback should be year-after-year. The guy was a numbers machine. Elway put the Broncos on his back the whole season and he was slowly becoming the best late-game situational player as a runner and passer the game has ever seen. Stat wise, Marino wins, yet if we're talking about who was more important to his team and the league, then Elway has to win that argument. (More important meaning -- Montana and Marino were already elite quarterbacks: winning/making Super Bowls, breaking passing records, making Pro Bowls and playing the position at a high level. Elway wasn't in the upper echelon yet, until he joined them at the top in '86). The league was better for it. The NFL had a new star on their hands. Plus, he did make the Super Bowl. **ELWAY**. Borderline.

1987: A 24-day strike by the players cut the 16-game season to 15. The 49ers returned to their elite ways going an NFL-best 13-2 and entered the postseason as the front-runners to win the Super Bowl. A main reason for that was the play of First Team All-Pro Montana and wide receiver Jerry Rice. Montana was in rare form in '87, tossing 3,054 yards and 31 TD passes to 13 INTs in only 13 games while Rice, set a then NFL-record, by catching 22 TD receptions. Due to the shaky defense and unreliable running game the Dolphins had, they failed to make the playoffs. Marino still had a Pro Bowl type season: 3,245 passing yards and 26 TD passes to 13 INTs. As for the quarterback from Denver, "Football fans, meet your 1987 NFL MVP... John Elway." Elway continued to improve as a dangerous passer to go along with his nimble scrambling capability. His numbers didn't amaze you but it didn't tell the whole story of how impressive Elway was in '87. He threw for 3,198 yards, 19 TDs, and ran for a career-high 304 yards and 4 rushing TDs. Most of all, his Broncos went an AFC-best 10-4-1. Elway's Broncos and Montana's 49ers were both the top seeds in their respected conferences and seemed primed to meet each other in Super Bowl XXII. When all the dust was settled, only Elway's Broncos would be playing in San Diego. Montana and the 49ers were shockingly upset at home by the Minnesota Vikings 36-24 in the Divisional Playoff game. What was more disturbing was Montana being replaced by backup, future Hall of Famer Steve Young midway through the game. It all seemed to be unraveling in San Francisco. Denver, by the way, was getting stronger as the playoffs went on. Denver pounded the Houston Oilers 34-10 behind Elway's 259 passing yards and 3 total TDs (2 pass, 1 run) and in one of the most exciting conference championship games in NFL history in a rematch versus the Browns, the Broncos prevailed 38-33 with Elway tossing 3 TD passes. By leading the Broncos to back-to-back AFC titles, Elway was enhancing his big game rep even more. Now he just needed to take care of business against Washington in the Super Bowl. The favored Broncos turned out to be no match for the Redskins on that day. Washington netted 602 total yards of offense and ran Denver out of the stadium 42-10. Overall, Elway just couldn't get the offense going, throwing for 257 yards, 1 TD pass and 3 INTs. For the second straight Super Bowl, the season ended ugly for Elway and the Broncos. The negatives outweighed the positives.

ADVANTAGE: Elway or Montana? Take your pick. Even though Elway was the MVP of the league, Montana did make First Team All-Pro over him (Elway made the Second Team). Montana led his team to the league's top record, though Elway lifted his team to the Big Game again, despite losing. Montana was spectacular in '87, although overall, Elway's responsibility to his team was far greater than Montana's and his play was a little bit more imposing, especially when it came down to the playoffs. (Unless, we're discussing Super Bowl XXII). This is probably even, but **ELWAY,** by a decimal point.

1988: In a way, this was an up-and-down season for all three. (Each player did not make the Pro Bowl). When the playoffs began, both Marino and Elway would be watching from their couches. Miami finished 6-10 and Denver 8-8. Funny how you make two straight Super Bowls and the sudden expectation is for that team to crawl right back in that position with ease, just because they were there the previous two years. That was the Denver Broncos for ya! To make matters worse, Elway was very precarious and shaky in '88. Slowed by injuries most of the year, Elway had a 17 to 19 touchdown passs-to-interception ratio and seemed to relapse back to the struggles in his early years. Marino had an OK season compared to the lofty standards the media/press had set for him. Montana, on the other hand, came into the season in a QB battle with Steve Young for who would receive more playing time. Young appeared in 11 games that year, but Montana regained the starting position full-time in the middle of the season and the 49ers finished 10-6, with a #2 seed in the NFC playoffs. In the Divisional Playoff game rematch with the Vikings, Montana threw 3 TD passes to Jerry Rice in a 34-9 win. In a freezing, cold NFC title game vs.

the Bears away, the 49ers were on point, cruising 28-3 behind another 3 TD pass game from Montana. In a tightly bound Super Bowl faceoff versus the AFC-best Cincinnati Bengals and league MVP, quarterback Boomer Esiason, this baby would go down to the wire. With the 49ers down 16-13 with 3:10 left on their own 8-yard line, Joe Cool went to work, leading San Fran on the most famous game-winning drive in Super Bowl history – 11 plays, 92 yards, and a perfectly thrown, back-of-the-end zone, 10-yard strike to wideout John Taylor with 34 ticks left to get by 20-16. It was the 49ers third title of the decade. Rice won MVP honors catching a Super Bowl record 11 balls and 215 receiving yards, and added to that with 1 TD catch. Montana was flawless once again, throwing for 357 yards, 2 TD passes and 0 INTs. Joe Cool showed once again nobody was better in the waning minutes of a close contest quite like him.

ADVANTAGE: Even though all three quarterbacks didn't have big seasons, this one isn't really up for discussion. Marino and Elway watched Montana collect his third Super Bowl. Enough said.
MONTANA.

1989: If you thought you saw the best of Joe Montana already, then think twice people! 1989 served as his finest year, leading a ridiculously stacked 49ers team to a league best record at 14-2. '89 Montana clicked on all cylinders. In 13 games played, he threw 3,512 yards, 26 TD passes, 8 INTs and had the highest quarterback rating in NFL History (112.4), up to that point. He won the NFL MVP, Offensive Player of the Year and was a First Team All-Pro. You can't have a better season than that (well a Super Bowl title would sure cap it off). Do I really have to mention Marino's Dolphins? If you guessed that Miami missed the playoffs for the fourth consecutive season, while Marino had a pretty good/decent year on his part, then you guessed right. You win the Grand Prize! As uneven and incoherent as Elway was in '89, he found some way to lead Denver to the AFC's top seed at 11-5. In yet another AFC title game matchup with Cleveland, Denver would once again top the Browns 37-21 led by Elway's 385 passing yards, 3 TD passes and 0 INTs. The 49ers glided to Super Bowl XXIV, squashing the Vikings 41-13 and the Los Angeles Rams 20-3, as Montana operated at an MVP-level. The Montana-Elway clash was on. Yes, Elway and the Broncos were playing well, but Montana and the 49ers were on the verge of going down as one of the best teams of all-time and were highly favored to do so. The Broncos best hope was that their top-ranked D could slow down the 49ers well-balanced offense and hope the game would be close, so Elway could win it for them at the end. Sadly for Denver, the plan didn't work. The game was a wipeout. San Francisco slaughtered

Denver 55-10 in the largest blowout in Super Bowl history. The 49ers dominated in every facet of the game, outgaining the Broncos in total yards 461 to 167, and they ended up forcing four turnovers to the 49ers none. Montana completely outclassed Elway in this one. Montana was remarkable, completing 22 out of 29 passes for 297 yards, throwing a then-record 5 TD passes, 0 INTs and won his third Super Bowl MVP award. Elway's performance at best was dismal. He scored the Broncos only touchdown, off a 3-yard run, but only completed 10 out of 26 passes for 108 yards, no TD passes, and 2 INTs. The major question surrounding Elway after the game was "Will he ever win a Super Bowl?" At the time, after three difficult Super Bowl losses, the answer appeared to be never. The 49ers finished the '80s as the "Team of the Decade" with four Lombardi trophies in their possession. As for Montana, go look at the cover of *Sports Illustrated* a week after they won the Super Bowl, with him on the front and the title in capital letters saying, "JOE KNOWS SUPER BOWLS." That's all you need to know about No. 16.

ADVANTAGE: Do I even need to debate this one? Alright, I didn't think so. All the way, **MONTANA.**

1990: Coming off back-to-back titles, Montana and the Niners were poised for a NFL record third consecutive Super Bowl championship. As special as Montana's 1989 season was, his 1990 campaign might have been more impressive. Once again, Montana led the Niners to the best regular season record at 14-2 and took home his second straight MVP trophy. Another great honor came Montana's way, when he was named 1990 *Sports Illustrated* Sportsman of the Year. The Broncos dropped to 5-11 and missed the postseason, with Elway having a mediocre season. Marino and the Dolphins bounced back and surged to a 12-4 record, only to be defeated by the ensuing AFC Champion Buffalo Bills in a second round shootout. The 49ers leaped into the playoffs clearly as the top dogs, although the quest for an unprecedented three-peat was cut short in the NFC title game against the soon-to-be Super Bowl champs New York Giants 15-13 in a defensive war. With the Niners clinging to a 13-9 lead early in the fourth quarter, Montana was hit hard in the back, suffered a concussion and a broken finger. He didn't return and San Francisco would lose by a field goal as time expired.

ADVANTAGE: As disappointing as it was to come up short three-peating, you still can't deny how splendid Montana was this season, once again. Unanimous Decision to **MONTANA.**

1991: In training camp, Montana suffered an elbow injury that sidelined him for the entire season. In his absence, San Francisco went 10-6 and missed the playoffs for the first time since 1982. After making the playoffs the previous year, Miami regressed right back to being pedestrian – missing the playoffs at 8-8 – while Marino did everything possible to carry his team to relevancy. Elway and the Broncos recovered from the terrible '90 season to go 12-4 and clinch a #2 seed in the AFC. Elway rode Denver all the way to the AFC title game, then falling to the Bills 10-7. It was another opportunity for Elway and another one that slipped through the cracks.

ADVANTAGE: Honestly, I can't say that anyone had an edge over the other this year, especially when Montana missed the whole season. But hey, since someone has to win (at least I think someone has to win), then **ELWAY** takes the cake for getting his team the farthest.

Montana wound up missing most of the 1992 season and only appeared in one game; the 49ers last regular season game on Monday Night Football, in which he performed brilliantly. With Montana getting older, he still showed he can be a starter and play at a high level; however at this point, Steve Young had replaced him. The 49ers, eager to hand over the reins to Young, ended up trading Montana to the Kansas City Chiefs during the offseason in April of 1993. Even at the tender age of 37, Montana still displayed he had the magic touch. Montana, along with newly acquired free agent star running back, Marcus Allen led the Chiefs to an 11-5 mark, good for a #3 seed in the AFC. The Chiefs put together two late-game comeback wins in the postseason only to fall in the conference title game to the Bills. In what would be Montana's last season in 1994, he sure left some indelible marks that would be highlights in his finale. In Week 2 against his former team the 49ers and Steve Young, the Chiefs came through 24-17. In a one-for-the-ages battle versus Elway on MNF in Week 7, Montana outdueled Elway in the final seconds in this see-saw affair, driving the Chiefs down the field with 1:29 left to throw the game-winning TD pass to lead Kansas City to victory 31-28. The Chiefs went 9-7 and in Montana's last game he was ousted by the Dolphins and his longtime rival, Dan Marino 27-17 in the Wild Card game. As for Marino, he would continue to play at an advanced level in the '90s (not quite at the level of the '80s), although his Dolphins teams at times were sometimes playoff-bound and other times plain subpar but at the end he never reached his goal of winning a Super Bowl.

Moving forward in the '90s, disappointment only seemed to follow the Broncos. They missed the playoffs in '94 and '95. In 1996, they went 13-

3 (tied for the best record with the Packers) and were in excellent position to get to the Super Bowl. Denver, who was favored by 14 points in the divisional round against the expansion Jacksonville Jaguars fell 30-27 and again went home contemplating where it all went wrong. The odds seemed to be stacked against Elway ever winning a title -- that is until 1997 came. Elway threw for a career-high 27 TD passes in '97 and out of nowhere, unexpectedly led the 12-4 Wild Card Broncos to Super Bowl XXXII. It was a rather surprising run for Denver. They knocked out both the No. 1 seed Chiefs in the second round and the No. 2 seed Steelers in the title game to advance to San Diego, where the reigning champion Packers and 3-time league MVP, Brett Favre were waiting. The Packers were a double-digit favorite and were deservingly so. Coming in, the Broncos, especially Elway, were haunted by their previous Super Bowl losses and a win would put all the critics to rest for both Elway and the Denver franchise. The game was close all the way to the end. The signifying moment of Elway's career came in the third quarter with the score tied at 17-17 and Denver facing a third & 6 on Green Bay's 12-yard line. Elway dropped to pass, couldn't find anyone, then took off scrambling, dove headfirst while three Packers defenders hit him so hard that he spun around in midair and landed past the first down marker to keep the drive alive. Two plays later, they punched in a touchdown and went on to a 31-24 win in one of the most memorable Super Bowls ever played. FINALLY AT LAST, Elway's quest for that elusive Super Bowl title was complete. Elway wasn't spectacular (12 out of 22 passes completed, 123 passing yards, no TD passes, 1 INT) but it was his guidance and willingness to do whatever it took to win that lifted Denver to their franchise's first championship. Denver's win snapped a 13 game-winning streak the NFC had over the AFC in the Super Bowl. The following year, the Broncos soared to an AFC-best 14-2 and returned back to the Super Bowl. Elway and Marino's only playoff encounter versus each other took place in the '98 Divisional Round, with Elway and the crew drubbing Marino and his boys 38-3. The Broncos went on to win consecutive titles after beating the Atlanta Falcons 34-19. Elway won game MVP honors, throwing for 336 yards, 1 TD pass, 1 INT and a rushing TD that put the game out of reach. At age 38, that was Elway's last game. Not a better way to leave the game than on top!

Marino vs. Montana! That was all the talk heading into Super Bowl XIX.

Wouldn't mind getting my hand on all three of those cards!

Elway against the Browns in the 1986 AFC Championship Game.

Joe tossing a pass vs. the Dolphins in Super Bowl XIX.

Dan "The Man" with that rifle arm.

"FINALLY, I got my hands on this trophy."

Joe and his four lovely championship rings.

The dude sure knew a thing about Super Bowls.

So, Who's Better- Here are the three quarterback's career highlights and awards…

Joe Montana
- 4 Super Bowl titles
- 3 Super Bowl MVPs
- 2 NFL MVPs
- 8 Pro Bowl Selections
- 3-time First Team All-Pro
- 3-time Second Team All-Pro
- 16-7 Playoff record
- Voted Starting Quarterback for 1980s All-Decade Team

Dan Marino
- No Super Bowl titles
- No Super Bowl MVPs
- 1 NFL MVP
- 9 Pro Bowl Selections
- 3-time First Team All-Pro
- 5-time Second Team All-Pro
- 8-10 Playoff record

John Elway
- 2 Super Bowl titles
- 1 Super Bowl MVP
- 1 NFL MVP
- 9 Pro Bowl Selections
- No First Team All-Pro
- 3-time Second Team All-Pro
- 14-7 Playoff record
- Voted Starting Quarterback for 1990s All-Decade Team

From the look of things, Montana's resume is certainly more accomplished than Elway's and Marino's. To some degree, that could be a knock against Montana (I will explain). Nice leg up for Joe but you can't settle a debate like this by just looking at their resume, now can you? Or maybe you can. When observing the historical context of each QB's career, there are these kind of questions or statements that appeared to flow around them regularly:

1.) How can John Elway be mentioned as one of the best quarterbacks ever, when his numbers for about half of his career were mediocre? Go see for yourself.

2.) Dan Marino was one hell of a quarterback but he never led his team to the promise land. Guess we're gonna have to put him on the infamous "Greatest Athletes Never to Win a Championship List" with guys like Ted Williams, Karl Malone, Elgin Baylor, Barry Bonds, Ty Cobb, Barry Sanders, etc.

3.) Joe Montana's teams were loaded. I bet if Marino and Elway played with the kind of Hall of Famer/Pro Bowl talent that Montana played with year-after-year, than they would have a bunch of rings on their fingers too.

Let's answer these bad boys head on…

1.) You're kinda right. If you were to look at Elway's numbers throughout his career without ever seeing him play, then you would probably think he was an average quarterback. Elway played 16 seasons. In his first eight seasons from 1983-1990, he averaged 16 TD passes to 16 INTs a season. Doesn't seem like Hall of Fame type numbers, huh? (You also can't forget that Elway played for one of the most conservative, uptight coaches ever in Dan Reeves. Maybe if he would have unleashed Elway more often, his numbers could have been bigger). In his last eight seasons from 1991-1998, he averaged 20 TD passes to 12 INTs a season. That's more like it! Fact is, Elway's numbers were better in the second half of his career than in the first half. Yes, Elway's stats were ordinary in his first eight years, yet that didn't tell the whole story with him. There are some athletes you can't fully judge how great they are by just looking at their stats. John Elway was one of those athletes. Elway was a one-man recking crew for Denver. What didn't show in his numbers, he made up for it with will and determination. He was unbelievably athletic, who when a play broke down, could make plays with his legs and cannonball arm that other quarterbacks couldn't make. Most importantly, through those first eight seasons, he always put Denver in a position to win and most of the time he delivered. I mean the dude got Denver to the Super Bowl three times in the '80s (all losses) by pretty much playing with inferior teammates. Elway carried the Broncos as far as he could take them in his first eight years. His numbers didn't say so but his play on the gridiron prominently impacted his team and he scared the living piss out of teams when the games got close. Nothing mediocre about that!

2.) Sure, we're gonna have to put Dan Marino on the list. Matter of fact, he's already on there. Marino never won a Super Bowl and when he's mentioned with the best quarterbacks of all-time, he's always in the discussion, however, that's as far as Marino gets in the debate. He's no doubt in the conversation, but is rarely referred as the G.O.A.T (Greatest of All Time). The "never winning a championship" tag *has* and *will* continue to stick with him and it's a shame too because it takes away the fact that Marino had all the tools you would want in a quarterback – size, powerful arm, good vision, got the football out on time, pocket presence, fearlessness, daring and an aggressive mindset. Marino was the prototypical quarterback. If I had a chance to take the clone of any QB in NFL history, I would take Marino's all day. He was that special. Was it his fought he never won a title? Ummm…Yes and No. That leads us to the last statement/question…

3.) For the most part of his career, Montana's 49ers teams *were* stacked. He played with a plethora of Hall of Famers/Pro Bowlers/superb players such as Jerry Rice, Roger Craig, John Taylor, Steve Young, Dwight Clark, Freddie Solomon, Tom Rathman, Bubba Paris, Ronnie Lott, Charles Haley, Bill Romanowski, Matt Millen, Eric Wright and Keena Turner. The 49ers were practically a championship-contending team every season in the '80s/early '90s and Joe was the ace commander of his troops. As for Elway and Marino…they simply can't say they played with those caliber of players in their early years and for much of their career. They were stranded on an island, left to fend for themselves. From 1983-1991, Elway played with a total of four offensive Pro Bowl players (running backs Sammy Winder in '84 and '86, Bobby Humphrey in '90 and Gaston Green in '91), who at their peak were average backs. It wasn't until 1992 (his 10th season) that he played with a Pro Bowl wide receiver or tight end -- Hall of Fame tight end Shannon Sharpe. In Elway's last few seasons, he was surrounded by better offensive players: All-Pro running back and formal NFL MVP Terrell Davis, Sharpe, and receivers Rod Smith and Ed McCaffrey that helped lead Denver to those two straight titles.

For 17 seasons in Miami, Marino never had a formidable defense or a strong, consistent running game (he played with only one 1,000-yard rusher; Karim Abdul-Jabbar in 1996). Miami's offense was never balanced; then again, Marino did have the terrific wide receiver duo of Mark Clayton and Mark Dupier for 10 seasons, who were constant Pro Bowlers and he had Hall of Famer Irving Fryar to throw to from 1993-1995. Miami's game plan pretty much was to have Marino chunk it 30-50 times a game and teams knew it was coming. That was their best chance to win. Their running game was completely abysmal and because of that, teams would stack eight men in the box to shut Marino down -- and at times he would still light them up. Marino and Elway both did the heavylifting for their franchises for years and the end results equaled continuous defeat and bitter frustration. Montana never had this problem, although you can't discount him for having great players around him. The one constant for the 49ers four Super Bowl teams was Montana. He was the driving force behind those teams. Who's the first player people think about or bring up when discussing the 49ers dynasty? Joe Montana is the answer. That's all you need to know!

In addition, I want to dismiss the myth that Montana had it made and walked in on a perfect situation with San Francisco. Go back and look at where the franchise was when he got drafted. The Niners were terrible in his first two seasons and suddenly in his third year they were Super Bowl champs. It wasn't a coincidence. Montana was the difference maker and the '81 Niners were nowhere as good as the '84, '88, and '89 squads. (Go look at the '81 roster and compare it to the other three teams if you don't believe me). What about Montana at age 37, carrying a less-heralded/solid Kansas City Chiefs team (not close to being in the same class as the '80s 49ers teams) all the way to the AFC Championship game in '93? That my friends is called having an influence! Yeah, maybe if you would have replaced Montana in San Francisco with Marino or Elway, it's possible to think they could have won more titles or just as many but in all actuality...you can't. It's inconceivable to even think about it. There's just no point. Montana displayed he can win with *both* superior and inferior teams. That was the true greatness of Joe Montana.

Glad I provided my two cents on those topics. Now let's try and put a conclusion on the debate of this trio. Of the three, Montana observed the field and read the defense the best; Marino was the best pure passer; and Elway was the best athlete. All-time: Montana is the most accurate QB ever (some say Tom Brady); Marino is the most prolific QB ever; and Elway is the best two-way QB ever (runner and passer). This sucker gets more difficult by the minute! One characteristic that Montana and Elway possessed that Marino lacked was the necessary leadership skills and intangibles. People forgot that Marino had more around him than Elway early in their careers (the "Marks Brothers" were two of the best wideouts in the game for a decade) and Elway still accomplished more with less than Marino did. (In my opinion, no quarterback did more with less talent in history than Elway, with Tom Brady coming in a close second). I feel as potent a passer as Marino was, he could have had a bigger effect on his teammates and that could have made the difference in Miami being more successful and possibly winning a Super Bowl. Elway and Montana's teammates loved them, revered them and would go to war for them. Not saying Marino's teammates wouldn't but not in the same way as his two rivals. When it comes down to the Elway-Marino argument, I'd rather have Elway on my side because I want him in a crucial moment or in an important game more than I want Marino. Yes, Elway's numbers were not as staggering as Marino's and when both quarterbacks were at their absolute best, Marino was certainly greater but Elway was superior to Marino when it came time to elevating his play and his teams play to a high level in the huge moments. A testament to that is not only Elway's two Super Bowl wins but his five Super Bowl appearances – tied for the most ever by a starting quarterback.

No quarterback in history embedded a better blend of being a winner, having clutch pedigree, excellent numbers, consistency season-after-season and leadership capabilities like Montana. When the stakes got higher, Montana was at his best. If you look up what the definition of clutch means, then Montana's name should be right next to it. He was that smooth. The assumption is Elway and Marino were more clutch than Montana because they have more career fourth quarter comebacks/game-winning drives (Marino 51 total, Elway 49 total) than Montana does. I say you're crazy. Montana had his share too (31 4th quarter comebacks) and he came through more often on the biggest stage than both his foes. Performing on the biggest stage was Montana's specialty. The main reason you have to put him over Elway and Marino is fairly simple – Montana beat both Elway and Marino in the Super Bowl. You know, when it mattered the most. He just didn't beat them, he out-Broadwayed them in both title games. (If you didn't catch on, it's short for outperformed. New York-style baby!). Remember in the Borg-Connors-McEnroe section, when I said Montana owned the Super Bowl? Well, he *owned* it alright. He was 4 for 4 in Super Bowls, finishing with 83 of 122 passes completed (68 percent) 1,142 passing yards, 11 TD passes, 2 rushing TDs and no INTs. Joe Cool played perfect football. (The crazy thing is he most likely should have won six Super Bowls instead of four. The '87 and '90 49ers finished with the league's best record and were the Team to Beat heading into the playoffs until both were unexpectedly defeated). To put it all in perspective, if the world was coming to an end and I had the choice of picking one quarterback in the history of the game to win one football game and save the world, I'm not thinking twice about it. I'm putting the football in the hands of Joseph Clifford "Joe" Montana, Jr. to save the universe.

My Rankings

1. Joe Montana
2. John Elway
3. Dan Marino

2. Muhammad Ali-Joe Frazier-George Foreman

This triad of fighters were the three greatest heavyweight boxers from the entire 1970s, declared the "Greatest Heavyweight Generation Ever." Muhammad Ali, Joe Frazier and George Foreman stood as the major stars and champions from that glorified decade of boxing but what distinguished this period as perhaps the finest era in the history of boxing of any weight class, was the depth of an immense number of great champions, respectable names, and worthy competitors. The list includes: Larry Holmes, Ken Norton, Leon Spinks, Oscar Bonavena, Jimmy Ellis, Floyd Patterson, Jerry Quarry, Earnie Shavers, Chuck Wepner, Ron Lyle, George Chuvalo, Jimmy Ellis, etc. With boxing being in a state of flux the last fifteen years, it's pretty easy to look back during that time and realize how gigantic the sport was compared to now. Translation: Sports fans had it made! Heavyweight boxing in the '70s was comparable to what the NBA was in the '80s, what the NFL was in the late '60s/1970s, what Major League Baseball was in the '50s, what College Basketball was in the 1980s/early '90s, and what golf was in the late '90s/2000s when Tiger was destroying his opponents and monopolizing golf courses. Boxing sat at the top of the sporting world and the key reasoning was because of the magnificent Ali-Frazier-Foreman rivalry that provided juicy headlines, never-ending buzz and legendary fights that will likely never be duplicated in heavyweight boxing ever again. Quite simply, Foreman, Frazier and Ali *were* the boxing establishment. Everything went through and around them.

One unique facet of all three boxers' career was that each of them became household names by winning an Olympic gold medal (Ali at the 1960 Olympics in Rome as a light heavyweight; Frazier at the 1964 Olympics in Tokyo as a heavyweight; and Foreman at the 1968 Olympics in Mexico City as a heavyweight), only Ali would be the first to get a crack at stardom. The Louisville, Kentucky native (named Cassius Clay at the time) showed early in his pro career that he was unlike any boxer or athlete the sport had ever seen. The 6-foot-3 Clay had an unusual style. Instead of holding his hands high to protect his face from punches, Clay carried his hands low, relying on his impeccable speed, quick footwork, and marvelous anticipation to duck and avoid punches to the head. Clay also displayed a wide number of explosive jabs and combinations that he used to perfection to end many of his fights early. As a young fighter (nicknamed "The Louisville Lip"), Clay developed a reputation for being a trash talker, boaster, self-promoter, poet and rhymer all rolled into one. He never shied away from the camera and the media soaked up every chance they could get to interview or cover him. He was a delight, controversial to cover (Just ask Howard Cosell and Dick Schaap), and throughout his career said many of the most audacious, clever and funny quotes the world has ever heard:

"I am the greatest, I said that even before I knew I was."

"When you are as great as I am, it is hard to be humble."

"If you even dream of beating me, you'd better wake up and apologize."

"I'm not the greatest; I'm the double greatest. Not only do I knock'em out, I pick the round."

(My personal favorite) "I'm so fast that last night I turned off the light switch in my hotel room and was in bed before the room was dark."

"I'll be floating like a butterfly and stinging like a bee."

"I am America. I am the part you won't recognize. But get used to me. Black, confident, cocky; my name, not yours; my religion, not yours; my goals, my own; get used to me."

"I'm young, I'm handsome, I'm fast, I'm pretty and can't possibly be beat."

...and he's got more where that came from! The man was the most flamboyant athlete we've ever seen. Young Cassius Clay was changing boxing and the way we look at sports in general and America had yet to even realize it.

Clay was rolling with a 19-0 record but his first big test would be on February 25, 1964 in Miami, Florida against the heavyweight champion Sonny Liston. Liston was being called the best heavyweight fighter since Joe Louis and not to mention 43 of 46 sports writers had Liston winning. When the fight began, it was apparent the 22-year-old Clay's speed and quick jabs were too much for the bigger, slower Liston and it resulted in a stunning upset, when Liston didn't come out for the 7th round due to a shoulder injury. He shocked the world and became the youngest heavyweight champion in history. The next day, Clay announced he was joining the Nation of Islam and changed his name to Muhammad Ali. Ali got a rematch with Liston in 1965 and ended the fight in the 1st round with the self-proclaimed "Phantom Punch" to defend his crown. Ali would defend his title nine times through 1967 with some overwhelming, high-class performances against quality fighters like Floyd Patterson, Henry Cooper, George Chuvalo, Cleveland "Big Cat" Williams and Ernie Terrell. His dismantling of Cleveland Williams was a pure masterpiece, with Ali showing the full package. No one could touch Ali…that is until the U.S. Military came calling. In 1967, with the Vietnam War occurring, the military attempted to draft Ali but he refused to be inducted due to his religious beliefs and disapproval of the war. He would be vilified by millions for this decision. Ali would later be stripped of his heavyweight title, his boxing license was suspended and he could not fight for three years. As his case went to the U.S. Supreme Court, support for Ali grew and he became a hero, an inspiration, and a symbol for young Americans, especially the black race – speaking at colleges and universities across the country to protest against the government and the war. In Ali's three-year banishment (1967-1970) from the ring, a slew of fighters vied for Ali's title, although the brawler from Philly, Joe "Smokin" Frazier would seize the belt in 1970 after beating WBA (World Boxing Association) champion, Jimmy Ellis to become the undisputed heavyweight champion of the world. The 5-foot-11 Frazier was known for his relentless bob-and-weave attack that used to apply swarming pressure on his opponents, and usually finished his victims off with his vicious left hook. In the same year, Ali would be reinstated back into boxing and would eagerly be looking to get back what was once his. Ali's comeback consisted of two successful wins over Jerry Quarry and Oscar Bonavena in 1970 and that soon paved the way for this showdown…

Ali-Frazier I

OH BABY! Talk about a matchup! It was all going down on March 8, 1971. The elements for this fight were downright fascinating:

Called, "The Fight of the Century"

Muhammad Ali, 31-0 (25 KOs) vs. Joe Frazier, 26-0 (23 KOs)

The Peoples Champion vs. The Heavyweight Champion

Undefeated Champ vs. Undefeated Champ

Anti-War Movement vs. Pro-War Movement

If you were black, young, and liberal, you rooted for Ali.

If you were white, upper-class, and conservative, you rooted for Frazier.

The biggest boxing fight ever in the biggest and greatest city in the U.S. (New York City) taking place at the most famous sports venue (Madison Square Garden) in America.

The build-up for this fight was incredible. The atmosphere was electric. This was a spectacle the sports world had never seen before. Three hundred million people watched on TV. There was an A-List Celebrity Crowd in attendance: Frank Sinatra, Cher, Woody Allen, Bing Crosby, Diana Ross, Dustin Hoffman, Burt Lancaster, Mia Farrow and others. This was like the Grammy's, Oscars, Super Bowl, NBA Finals and World Series combined together. This fight mixed the best of Hollywood with the best of sports. In my opinion and to many, Frazier-Ali I *was* and *still* is the most hyped, significant, anticipated, exciting sporting event in sports history. (You can tell how giddy I would have been if I was attending this fight. High as a kite brother!) The reason being because of how great these two boxers were. The 27-year-old Frazier was in his boxing prime, looking to punish the former heavyweight champion for all his "Uncle Tom" remarks/insults, and prove he was the real heavyweight champ. The 29-year-old Ali was coming back from a 3 ½ year absence (we still didn't know how rusty he was from the layoff), carrying Black America on his shoulders and looking to show he was still the best. The boxing scene in the ring before the fight was gorgeous. Ali was wearing bright red trunks with a white waistband and Frazier was in light green trunks with the waistband color being yellow. To our gladness, the fight exceedingly lived up to the hype. Ali came out striking in the early rounds with rapid-quick jabs but Frazier came back responding in the middle rounds with numerous left hooks and blows to the body. As the fight went on, Ali started to become weary and Frazier kept attacking with continuous pressure. Ali kept the fight close heading into the 11th round, up until Smokin Joe gave Ali a nasty left hook that knocked him into the ropes. Ali got back up, however from there on Frazier took control of the fight and in the 15th round, Frazier landed another devastating left hook to Ali's jaw that sent him on his back. Ali managed to finish the fight; however Frazier walked away with a 15-round unanimous decision and retained his heavyweight title. It was Ali's first loss of his pro career and even more it was a defeat for all of the African-American community that was behind him. There was more to come from these two. Stay tuned.

After "The Fight of the Century" victory over Ali, Frazier successfully defended his title twice and seemed invincible. What Frazier didn't know was that on the day of January 22, 1973 in Kingston, Jamaica his reign on top of boxing would come crashing down... and fast. I present to you...

Frazier-Foreman I

Entitled "The Sunshine Showdown," Joe Frazier marched into Jamaica as the undisputed, undefeated heavyweight champion of the world at 29-0 (25 KOs). His opponent, George Foreman was a 6-foot-4 giant who amassed a record of 32-0 (29 KOs) and was the #1 challenger by the WBA and WBC. Foreman was literally a ferocious beast in the ring. He might have been the strongest, biggest and most intimidating heavyweight of all-time. His hard-hitting prowess walloped and dazed his victims. At the time, boxing experts were calling Foreman the hardest hitting heavyweight boxer since Sonny Liston and some thought he was even a harder puncher than The Big Bear. That was enough to get Frazier's attention. Smokin Joe was the favorite, granting it made no difference in the fight. With only two minutes into the first round, Frazier was knocked down. Foreman knocked Frazier down a total of six times within two rounds before the fight was stopped. That quickly, Frazier lost the title and Foreman was the new heavyweight champion. The mixture of Foreman's deluxe size, extended reach and power was far too much for Frazier to handle. It was a complete termination by Foreman and one of the top championship fight performances in boxing history.

Ali came back from his first loss and responded with 10 wins in a row before losing in a 12-round decision in March 1973 to the talented, hard fought Ken Norton (the most underappreciated, great heavyweight of that era) who famously broke Ali's jaw. Six months later, Ali won the rematch over Norton in another 12-round split decision and that set up...

Ali-Frazier II

The second battle between Ali-Frazier took place on January 28, 1974 in New York City at Madison Square Garden (same location as the first fight). The second fight wasn't as memorable and didn't quite live up to the standards of the first fight; nonetheless the fight was still worth the price of admission. Even though this was a non-title fight, there was still plenty on the line for both boxers. The winner of this fight would determine who would get the chance to dethrone the new heavyweight champion of the world, George Foreman. Frazier was eager to get another shot at Foreman and get the title back, while Ali sought to do the same but most critically he wanted to avenge his loss to Frazier from the first bout. Ali started off fast, quick on his feet, and clicking with his lightning speed combinations, pushing Frazier to the ropes. Ali continued to control the fight, throwing and landing more punches than Frazier. In rounds eight and nine, Frazier crept back in it, pinning Ali to the ropes with frenetic body shots until Ali started trading punches with Frazier and that led to Ali winning a clear 12-round unanimous decision and getting revenge against his archrival. Many sportswriters, who scored the fight, thought that Frazier should have won, but despite their opinion, Ali was moving on to get an opportunity at snagging the world title back in his possession.

In his second title defense in March 1974 as the newly-crowned Heavyweight King, Foreman found himself matched up against the always-dangerous Ken Norton (30-2 record heading into the fight) but Big George made quick work of Norton, nailing his opponent with powerful, mighty punches that ended the fight after two rounds. Now were going to Kinshasa, Zaire for…

Foreman-Ali

This wasn't just a boxing match, it was truly an extraordinary sports event that took place on October 30, 1974 promoted as "The Rumble in the Jungle." The events that occurred before and after the fight were so notorious and gripping that 22 years later in 1996, the bout was portrayed in an Academy Award winning documentary *When We Were Kings*. The 25-year-old heavyweight champion Foreman (40-0, 37 KOs) stormed into Zaire as a monster favorite over the 32-year-old Ali (44-2, 31 KOs). No one and I can't stress this enough, NO ONE gave Ali a chance of winning. (It seemed like the sports media, to me, gave Ali an even slimmer chance of beating Foreman than when he fought Liston in their first duel). A number of boxing analysts continuously mentioned how Ali barely beat both Frazier and Norton in his last fights with them, while Foreman drubbed both Norton and Frazier. The odds were stacked against Ali and he knew it, although that didn't stop him from his usual trash talk before the fight saying, "You think the world was shocked when Nixon resigned? Wait till I whump George Foreman's behind." Right from the beginning, the Zaire crowd was on Ali's side chanting emphatically, "Ali Bomaye" and he would feed off that liveliness in the 1st round, aggressively attacking Foreman with his superior punching speed, surprising the heavyweight champ. Ali knew Foreman's obvious weakness was his lack of quickness and his inability to last long in a fight. (Most of Foreman's fights to that point never went past three rounds). Ali got some shots off on Foreman but failed to seriously hurt him, while Foreman crept back in the bout at the end of the first round. The second round started with Ali changing his tactics up, retreating to the ropes, where his plan was to wear out the bigger Foreman by covering his head as he allowed Foreman to exert all of his energy by punching himself out. Ali's strategy continued: stay on the ropes, taunt Foreman vigorously to the point where he would get frustrated, absorb numerous big blows to the body (instead of the head) and when the opportunity presented itself – come in on Foreman with sharp straight-shot punches to the face. As the fight went on, Foreman failed to connect any clean shots to Ali's chin and by the time the seventh round ended – it was pretty clear Foreman was exhausted. Ali's "Rope-a-Dope" style was working and in the eighth round, he finished Foreman off with a ghastly left-right combination that knocked him to the deck. Ali had done it! (You have to remember that during Foreman's training in Zaire, he suffered a cut above his eye that not only pushed the fight back for a month, but it deeply affected his training regimen leading up to the match). In one of the massive upsets in boxing history, Ali regained the heavyweight title belt and soon went from being the most hated and vilified athlete in the world to the most heroic and beloved athlete. Quite a reversal, don't you say! After years of boasting that he was "The Greatest", if there was ever a fight in Ali's career that convinced you that he was The Greatest, then it was surely this one. As for Foreman – he was never the same after this crushing defeat.

Coming off beating Frazier in their second fight and amassing the heavyweight crown away from Foreman in a 10-month span, Ali was awarded the 1974 *Sports Illustrated* Sportsman of the Year. Ali was so popular and such an astounding figure in America in '74, that he was invited to the White House by Gerald Ford to shake hands with the President himself. In 1975, Ali defeated three competent fighters (Chuck Wepner, Ron Lyle, Joe Bugner) all in close-run bouts, while Frazier recovered from his loss to Ali by knocking out Jerry Quarry and Jimmy Ellis in becoming the #1 heavyweight challenger for Ali's title. To Manila, Philippines we go for...

Ali-Frazier III

The Thrilla in Manila! (Gotta love that title!) The Thrilla in Manila baby! (Sorry, I had to say it again folks. It just sounds too good). This was not only the third and final fight in the illustrious trilogy between Muhammad Ali (48-2, 35 KOs) and Joe Frazier (32-2, 27 KOs) but the climax to this heated rivalry. Ali, as the favorite came into the fight loose, free, confident and believed his opposition was washed up and looking for one last payday. While Ali took his training lightly and ran around town with the beautiful model, Veronica Porsche (while still married), Frazier was training with robust intensity and a sturdy purpose. Ali's "gorilla" remarks towards Frazier infuriated him and even more intensified Frazier's sour hatred for Ali. When Ali was promoting the fight during a press conference, he constantly punched a rubber gorilla, which was meant to represent Frazier while reputedly saying, "It's gonna be a thrilla, and a chilla, and a killa, when I get the Gorilla in Manila." The fight started with temperatures impending up to 100 degrees and the world on the verge of witnessing a titanic clash that would never forget. Ali came out looking to end the fight early and in the beginning it looked like he would do so. Ali won the early rounds, using his accustomed dancing style and diligently attacking Frazier with his distinct combinations, knocking him off-balance several times. Ali grew frustrated in the early rounds as he tried to knock Frazier out but Frazier refused to go down, instead turning up the heat in the 4th round by punishing Ali with shots to the body and right/left hooks to the head. Frazier took the middle rounds; gaining control of the fight with a flurry of punches, left hooks and great use of his smothering fighting style. Frazier's training was paying off as Ali began to tire, although in the 10th round, Frazier was the one slowing down. In the 11th round, Ali afflicted his most damage on Frazier – using his speed to get around and jab at will on Frazier, which bruised his face and left serious swelling to his eyes. Ali continued to go after Frazier and overwhelm him, who could not see out of one eye. It was the 13th round and Ali prolonged the assault to Frazier's eyes with one combination after another. Frazier was utterly blind when he stepped out for the 14th round and Ali once more punished him with more blows. Up to this point, both boxers were severely wounded and exhausted. Ali had just enough to come out for the 15th round, while Frazier was in no condition to continue. Before the 15th round, Frazier's trainer Eddie Futch, fearing the worse and seeing that his guy was too beaten to finish the bout -- stopped the fight giving Ali the victory in 14 grueling rounds in arguably the greatest boxing fight in the history of the sport. All you need to know to realize how destructive this duel was on both boxers was the comment Ali said after the fight, "This was the closest I ever felt to death." Luckily for Ali and Frazier, there never was a fourth fight because if there ever was, based on how these two battled against each other; death might have come their way in the ring. After losing the heavyweight belt to Ali in 1974, Foreman was inactive for all of 1975 but returned in 1976 looking to get a rematch with Ali. In Foreman's first fight back, he KO'd Ron Lyle in five rounds and for his next bout...

Foreman-Frazier II

In 1976, Frazier (32-3) wanted another attempt at beating Foreman (41-1), after Foreman's one-sided victory in 1973 and he got it. Given Frazier had not fought since the punishment he dished out and took from Ali a year later in Manila, he wasn't expected to have much of a chance in this fight. Frazier was on the downside of his career and early showed that the second fight between the two would be more competitive than the first. Frazier's quick head movement was the key in the beginning, dodging and avoiding Foreman's big shots – granted Foreman waited patiently, eventually clubbing Frazier with two mega punches in the fifth round. Next thing we knew, the fight was stopped and Frazier retired after the fight.

With Frazier out of the game (he did make a brief comeback in 1981: a 10-round draw against Floyd "Jumbo" Cummings), Ali continued to pluck away – defeating Ken Norton on September 1976 in a 15-round decision at Yankee Stadium in the conclusion of their spectacular, close-knit trilogy. He then loss the heavyweight title in February 1978 to Leon Spinks, and seven months later defeated Spinks in a rematch to regain the heavyweight championship for a record third time. It was his last victory. Meanwhile, Foreman never got another shot at Ali but after a 12-round loss to Jimmy Young – Foreman turned his life completely around. Big George became a born-again Christian and while he didn't officially retire from boxing, he dedicated the next decade to becoming an ordained minister for God. He returned to the ring in 1987 at age 38, and in 1994, Foreman did the impossible at the age of 45 and became the oldest heavyweight champion ever, knocking out the current champion Michael Moorer in Las Vegas. Everyone, The Golden Age of Heavyweight Boxing. What a thrilling ride it was!

Ali-Frazier I. What a scene it was.

The battle was on between Ali and Frazier.

Heavyweight Champion Joe Frazier and Challenger George Foreman have a stare off in 1972 during the weigh-in before their heavyweight title bout.

Foreman had his way against Frazier in their first fight.

Ali defeated Frazier in the second fight of their trilogy.

Ali and Foreman tumbling during the
"Rumble in the Jungle" fight.

The epic Thrilla in Manila fight.

The three finest heavyweights of their time.

So, Who's Better- Without a doubt, Ali, Frazier and Foreman are three of the ten greatest heavyweight boxers of all-time. All three conquered and were heavyweight champions in the strongest, most competitive and stellar era in boxing history. Ali was the most famous boxer, not only of the trio but in the history of the sport. Frazier was the toughest and most resilient. Foreman was a menace, the more physically imposing boxer. Ali had the best footwork and was the fastest heavyweight ever. Frazier produced the single best punch amongst his rivals, his ill-famed left hook. Foreman was in all probability the hardest puncher. What sticks out to me was how durable Ali was throughout his career. He could take a punch better than any heavyweight, lasted longer than Frazier and Foreman in fights and always seemed to come through victorious in bouts that would go the distance. You can't teach that ability. While Ali's endurance was a strength for him, it proved to be Foreman's downfall. Listen, Big George was as frightening of a force as we've ever seen in the ring. His opponents were literally scared of the man before the first bell would go off. Saying that, Foreman's lack of endurance and stamina killed him versus Ali. Before Foreman fought Ali, he was so used to belting his opponents in the early rounds and ending fights swiftly that when Ali pushed him into the middle rounds and beyond, Foreman just couldn't pace himself and keep up. In that fight, Foreman was punching himself out without even realizing it. If you think about it, Ali was a bad matchup for Foreman. Ali preyed on bigger/slower fighters that could not keep up with his outstanding speed, and quick head and feet movement. Also, Ali doesn't get enough credit for being a smart boxer. He could beat you with his amazing talent and his head. (Example: The Rope-a-Dope tactic he used on Foreman was pure genius). As we saw after that, Foreman wasn't the same. Mentally, he just checked out. The whole world thought Foreman was unbeatable including himself; however, when Ali knocked him on his butt, his invincibility forever vanished. There have been rumors that Foreman wanted another go at Ali but Ali declined. I think it was the total opposite -- Foreman wanted no part in a rematch. His confidence was too broken to fight him again. Why fight someone when you don't believe you can beat them and your confidence level is at an all-time low? That's why I think we never saw a second bout.

On the other hand, Foreman absolutely *owned* Frazier. You know the old saying "Styles make fights." Well, Frazier's aggressive style was no match for the sucker punches Foreman had waiting for him. The swarming/coming forward approach just didn't work against Foreman because of his sheer size, long reach and jaw-dropping shots to the head, whenever Frazier came in too close. Foreman's power overwhelmed Frazier in both fights and really, when you watch both fights, it was simply no contest. What failed versus Foreman, worked mightily well against Ali. Frazier gave Ali fits in all three fights because he pressured, smothered, and swarmed him constantly and that prevented Ali from containing the tempo and outboxing Frazier. Another issue Ali had was that he would too often drop his hands and that allowed Frazier to attack with jabs and left hooks. Given that, Ali prevailed two out of three times against Frazier. (Many believe the second fight Ali won, should have been a draw). Look, the two will always be intertwined together and their fights were as epic and nostalgic as any rivalry in sports history. Granted, when it comes to rivalries... Someone's gotta win it, right? Yep, Ali wins this. What propelled Ali over Frazier in the late rounds of their second and third fight was the whole repertoire he possessed: the blinding speed, coming forward to attack with profound left-right combinations, the ability to take all kinds of punches, well-conditioned to last long in fights, aptitude for repetitively wearing down his opponent, and unparalleled will and determination to finish his challenger off before they finish him. Ali and Frazier's battles were brutal, well-fought and very difficult to determine who the winner was; still, the all-around package Ali owned that no other boxer before him and since him in any weight class, was the difference in him inking it out twice versus Frazier.

Alright, here are the head-to-head records versus one another...

Frazier- 1-2 vs. Ali, 0-2 vs. Foreman

      1-4 combined record

Foreman- 2-0 vs. Frazier, 0-1 vs. Ali

      2-1 combined record

Ali- 2-1 vs. Frazier, 1-0 vs. Foreman

      3-1 combined record

Ali posted a winning record against his two biggest rivals. Head-to-head matchups are essential and vastly critical in rivalries when dissecting "Who's Better" or "Who won the rivalry", and Ali has the deciding factor working in his favor. Still don't think The Peoples Champ has the edge over Smokin Joe and Big George? Let's observe their career resumes.

As you will see, Ali defeated every top heavyweight fighter in his era. While Foreman and Frazier did beat a good number of quality/excellent fighters, they clearly didn't overthrow nowhere near as many high-class foes as Ali did. (Just to clarify, I'm talking strictly boxers from the '60s and '70s.)

Ali- Frazier (two), Foreman, Ken Norton (two), Floyd Patterson (two), Sonny Liston (two), Archie Moore, Jerry Quarry (two), Leon Spinks, Earnie Shavers, George Chuvalo (two), Ernie Terrell, Ron Lyle, Bob Foster, Mac Foster, Oscar Bonavena, Cleveland Williams, Zora Folley, Joe Bugner, Chuck Wepner, Jimmy Ellis, Jimmy Young, Doug Jones, Henry Cooper (two)

Foreman- Frazier (two), Ken Norton, George Chuvalo, Ron Lyle, Chuck Wepner

Frazier- Ali, Oscar Bonavena, Doug Jones, George Chuvalo, Jerry Quarry (two), Jimmy Ellis (two), Bob Foster, Joe Bugner

(FYI: Frazier never fought Norton. How did this fight not ever happen? Shaking my head in disappointment.)

That's an off-the-chart resume for Ali. He beat the best during the toughest heavyweight era in boxing history. Can't say enough about that!

Ali wins that round but Foreman compiled a better career win-loss record than Ali and Frazier...

Foreman- 76-5 (68 KOs)

Ali- 56-5 (37 KOs)

Frazier- 32-4 (27 KOs)

(As a reminder, Ali's record could have easily been more immense, if not for being banned from the ring for 3 ½ years.)

Another Note: It's peculiar how a large portion of fans mostly remember Ali from the '70s and not the '60s (before his exile), when he was in his prime. I can't recall a boxer who was more explosive and dominant than Ali was from 1964-1967. (If you wanted to pick Joe

Louis' run from 1939-1941, when he defended his heavyweight title 13 consecutive times, then I wouldn't argue.) Just imagine if we had a time machine – pulled '66 Ali, '71 Frazier and '73 Foreman out of it (when all three were at their peak and heavyweight champion of the world) and had them all fight each other. OH MAN, talk about compelling stuff. You'd be a damn fool to miss that action! (And yes, I'm still holding out hope we find this supernatural time machine one day. Keep your fingers crossed sports world.)

Now to settle the score, I have to declare that Joe Frazier was the best pound-for-pound heavyweight champion of all-time and Foreman winning the heavyweight title at age 45 (when evidently overweight and not in boxing shape) is as remarkable of an accomplishment that any boxer or athlete could attain, but still, it doesn't match what Ali achieved. He Shocked the World by defeating Liston, did the Unthinkable beating Foreman, and was the first three-time heavyweight champion. No disrespect to the likes of Joe Louis, Sugar Ray Robinson, Henry Armstrong, Jack Johnson, Jack Dempsey, etc., but when Ali kept telling the world he was The Greatest", The Louisville Lip was absolutely correct – He was the Greatest.

My Rankings

1. **Muhammad Ali**
2. **George Foreman**
3. **Joe Frazier**

1. Michael Jordan-Larry Bird-Magic Johnson

The NBA's Holy Trinity: Michael, Larry and Magic. If there has ever been three players from one sport during and after their playing days that *were* and still *are* synonymous with that sport/league, then it's definitely – Michael Jordan, Larry Bird, Magic Johnson and the NBA. Those three players and professional basketball will forever be linked and we humbly thank them for it. When we say No. 23, No. 32 and No. 33 changed the game, then we're not overexaggerating because THEY DID CHANGE THE GAME OF BASKETBALL! Words can't describe how much they meant to the game:

They simply made the game pure again.
We idolized and were inspired by them all at once.
It wasn't just a privilege to watch them play, it was an honor.
When we watched them live or on TV, it wasn't just a game – it was an event.
We savored every chance we got to see them perform.
When viewing the trio, we weren't just tuning into the game; they made you feel a part of it.
They produced thrills and moments on the court that made you feel like you were the luckiest person in the world...
and believe me – you were.

Magic, Jordan and Bird are a classic example of three preeminent leading actors in an Oscar-winning blockbuster drama movie. Think *The Departed* with Jack Nicholson, Leonardo DiCaprio and Matt Damon as the star actors. They were more than basketball superstars: Jordan, Magic and Bird were celebrities, sports legends, universal icons, big-name personalities, champions and megastars all varied together. Bird operated in Boston; Magic in Los Angeles; and Jordan in Chicago: Three historically great U.S. cities. Bird starred for the Celtics, Magic for the Lakers and Jordan for the Bulls. Currently No. 1, No. 2, and No. 3 (Celtics 17, Lakers 16, Bulls 6) in franchises with the most NBA championships won all-time. Bird ran the East Region; Magic seized the West Region; and Jordan controlled the Midwest Region. To put it quite simply: During the early 1980s to the early 1990s (the greatest period in NBA History), this threesome were frankly conquering over the basketball world but also the whole sports world. The galaxy was at their fingertips.

Yes the Bird-Jordan-Magic trio did transform the NBA into a worldwide phenomenon but it was the competition amongst one another, the greatness of each player, the performances from each player and their respective teams, and the undeniable success these three obtained during the '80s and '90s that put them on a mammoth pedestal. Now if you don't have any questions, I'm shifting this debate to my familiar year-by-year breakdown of the trio starting from 1984 (Bird and Magic's first Finals matchup and Jordan's last collegiate season) to 1992 (Magic already retired, Bird's final year and Jordan at his utmost best). Alright, let's get this show on the road.

1984: Up until this point (going into their fifth season), Magic had won two titles ('80 and '82) and Bird one ('81) but they had yet to meet in the championship series. That would all change in '84. After being the MVP runner-up for the last three years (1981-1983), Bird (24.2 ppg, 10.1 rpg, 6.6 apg) took home the trophy, while leading the Celtics to a league-best 62-20 record. For Magic (17.6 ppg, 13.1 apg, 7.3 rpg), this was the first season he was in full charge of the team at point guard (given he shared point guard duties with Norm Nixon in his first four seasons but he was swapped before the season for young Byron Scott), and with the extra responsibility on Magic's shoulders – Showtime was never better. A Celtics-Lakers Finals would finally come upon us after the matchup came so close to happening the last four years...

1980- Lakers win the West; Celtics lose in the East Finals

1981- Celtics win the East; Lakers upset in the first round

1982- Lakers win the West; Celtics lose in the East Finals

1983- Lakers win the West; Celtics lose in the second round

The Lakers-Celtics 1984 Finals standoff was what we all expected, envisioned, and wanted for years and at last, WE GOT IT. The series lived up to the hype and billing that we projected it would be. The Lakers won game 1 on the road. With the Lakers looking ready to grab a 2-0 series lead at the end of game 2, a bad pass by James Worthy led to a crucial steal and layup by Celtic guard Gerald Henderson that sent the game into overtime, where Boston would squeeze it out. Game 3 back in Los Angeles was an offensive assault by the Lakers. A 137-104 butt slapping. Young fellas growing up and getting into basketball, if you want to see Showtime at its finest, then game 3 exemplified what it was all about. Go to YouTube and check it out. A total work of art. Game 4 might have been the most dramatic and exhilarating finals game ever, with both teams playing at a profound level. Going down the stretch with the game tied at 125 and Boston with the ball, they would go to Bird with Magic switching off his man to guard him. What better way to finish maybe the best Finals game of all-time, than with Magic and Bird matching up against each other at the end. Bird got the ball with his back turned to the basket a few feet from the low-post block and nailed a turnaround jumper right in front of Magic. A few minutes later with a steal and dunk by Celtics M.L. Carr, the game was sealed. Game 5 back at Boston, known as the "Heat Game" had both teams playing under 97 degrees heat without any air conditioning and turned out to be one of Bird's best. The scorcher apparently didn't affect Bird, as he punched in 34 points and 17 rebounds and helped Boston snag the win. L.A. responded back winning a close game 6 back at The Forum behind a 30 pts-10 rebs showing by Kareem. Game 7 at Boston Garden turned out to be the clincher for Bird and the Celtics. Down the wire in game 7, the Celtics had all the answers and capitalized off errant Lakers mistakes. The Celtics showed they were the stronger, more physical and the mentally tougher team throughout the series -- and that prevailed. Bird won the Finals MVP honors (averaging 27.4 ppg, 14.0 rpg, 3.6 apg) and showed the world why many believed he was the best player in the game. Magic had a very good series (putting in 18.0 ppg, 13.6 apg, 7.7 rpg) and dished out a Finals record 95 assists for the series, but what hurt Magic was the poor late-game execution in game 2, the missed free throws and bad passes thrown in game 4, and the awful ball-handling/passing issues in game 7. Magic's late-game woes led to him being called "Tragic Johnson" by Celtic fans, some Celtic players (M.L. Carr and Cedric Maxwell especially), and the media during and after the Finals. It was a tough one to swallow for Magic as the loss pained him all summer. For Bird, he would savior this championship victory over Magic and the Lakers for a long, long time. Meanwhile, the collegiate Michael Jordan in his junior year and final year at UNC was showing us a sneak preview of what we were about to witness in the pros. He was a First Team All-American that won a handful of awards that season (ACC Player of the Year, Oscar Robertson Trophy, Naismith Player of the Year, Adolph Rupp Trophy and the John R. Wooden Award). He was also the leading scorer on the Olympic gold medal-winning USA team at the 1984 summer games. Jordan came out in '84 and was the third pick in the most ballyhooed NBA Draft in history. Little did we know that Young Jordan was about to take us on a spine-tingling journey.

UPPER HAND: Can UNC Jordan qualify for this honor, even though he was in college? Sorry, not this time. If Magic and Bird had subpar seasons (they didn't) and did not meet in a classic finals (they did), then I would say yes but that's not the case here. This is the pros young buck! Watch and learn! Both Magic and Bird separated themselves from players like Kareem, Dr. J, Moses, Moncrief, B. King, and Isiah as the two superlative players in basketball in '84 and the power command would continue for years to come, however Bird has to get the edge over Magic. Bird was the league MVP, Finals MVP, led the Celtics to the best record and most of all beat and outplayed Magic in the Finals – most notably at the end of games. **BIRD** takes it.

1985: "From North Carolina, at guard, 6-foot-6, M-I-C-H-A-E-L J-O-R-D-A-N!" (I had to reenact the Bulls introduction lineups from the late '90s. Couldn't help myself). His Airness was born! Michael Jordan stormed onto the professional basketball scene with a flurry. His moves, his athleticism, his balance, his dunks, his ability to fly and hang, his style, his swagger and his professionalism was unlike anything we've ever seen before by a player. Jordan became an instant hit in Chi-Town, even in away games. He won Rookie of the Year honors putting up 28.2 ppg on 51.5% shooting and was a starter in the All-Star Game (a rare feat for a rookie) but it didn't result in success for Chicago – as they were bounced in the first round of the playoffs. Once again, Bird's Celtics and Magic's Lakers were ahead of the field and it wasn't even close. From start to finish, both teams appeared to be in an all-out dash to see who would finish with the best record and grab home-court advantage throughout the playoffs. The Celtics won the marathon posting a league-best 63-19 record, just beating out the Lakers at 62-20. The key cog on both juggernauts functioning was the all-around, spectacular play of their two franchise players. Bird and Magic's squads were not only in the running for Best Regular Season Team, but both stars were the two leading candidates for the Most Valuable Player Award. Larry Legend came first, as the Magic Man finished second. Bird's '85 season might have been the best of his career. He poured in 28.7 ppg (second in the league), 10.5 rpg (eighth in the league), 6.6 apg, shot .52% from the field, and .42% from three-point range. Bird's signature game that season was his 60-point game outburst versus the Hawks that will be remembered for ages. Magic's '85 season can best be described as liberation and redemption. Magic averaged 18.3 ppg, 12.6 apg, 6.2 rpg, and played this season with one purpose and one purpose only of getting back to the Finals to claim the championship they let slip away the previous year. Both teams were on a collision course the entire season and the rematch would be on. The Lakers swooped in the NBA Finals with an 11-2 record and playing flawlessly, while the Celtics came in at 11-4. Heading into the Finals, it was no longer a 2-2-1-1-1 format but now a 2-3-2 setup. Knowing that, the Celtics had home-court advantage for the second year in a row. To say the Lakers got blown out in Game 1 was an understatement. It was more like assassinated. A dynamite effort from Boston resulted in a 148-114 demolition. After this game, the media thought the Lakers were through and were ready to anoint the Celtics as repeat champions. As Lee Corso would say best," Not so fast my friends." L.A. bounced back; winning four of the next five games to win the title in the game 6 clincher at Boston Garden behind the resurgent performance of series MVP Kareem Abdul-Jabbar (25.7 ppg, 9.0 rpg, 5.2 apg, 1.5 bpg), playmaking talent of James Worthy (23.7 ppg), and the leadership and focus of Johnson (18.3 ppg, 14.0 apg, 6.8 rpg, 2.5 spg). Victory could not have been sweeter for L.A., especially for Magic. The Lakers and Magic played this season with a mission and the end outcome was mission completed. No better feeling.

UPPER HAND: Jordan's first season was breathtaking and one of the more prolific rookie seasons in NBA History, although it doesn't match or come close to what Larry and Magic did in '85. For this season, I kinda feel obliged to draw even for #33 and #32. It's that deadlocked. Bird led Boston to the league's best record. Magic led Los Angeles to the league's second-best record. Bird won the league MVP. Magic was MVP runner-up. They both were NBA All-First Team. They both were in their primes and were at their unquestionable top form all season long. So when a debate like this is equal, what's the tiebreaker? Oh yeah, that's right – Winning. Magic and Bird's overall Finals performance was at best a draw, yet Magic was the one carrying the Lakers past Bird and the Celtics in the championship series and moved ahead of Bird with 3 titles to his rivals, 2. I desperately wanted to go even here, but **MAGIC** by a hairball.

1986: Going into the season, basketball fans, the media, sportswriters, broadcasters, and every one that associated some part of their life and time to the NBA, expected a third straight Boston-Los Angeles NBA Finals. It had become the norm in professional basketball. When June arrived, we expected to see one team in green and white and the other in purple and gold running up and down the court against each other. If we didn't, then we were taken aback by it and dissatisfied. Well, the sports world was surely shocked when we didn't get our presumed Finals. Once more, the Lakers and Celtics were ahead of the pack and the favorites heading into the postseason. The '86 Celtics were something special. I don't know if there has ever been a single-season team that meshed and had the chemistry that these guys had when they played together. Along with the Lakers, they made basketball an art form. The great frontcourt of Bird, McHale and Parish carried the C's to the league's best record for the third year running at an overbearing 67-15, including an NBA-record 40-1 home mark. The always incisive Bird (25.8 ppg, 9.8 rpg, 6.8 apg, .49 FG%, .42 3PT%, .89 FT%) put up another huge season and captured his amazing third consecutive MVP, joining Bill Russell (1961-1963) and Wilt Chamberlain (1966-1968) as the only players to win the award three times in a row. The Celtics first round opponent would be the 30-52 Chicago Bulls and their upstart guard. Jordan's sophomore season was cut short, only playing in 18 games due to a broken foot but he recovered at season's end and in time for the playoffs. Jordan would show the world he was on the cusp of superstardom -- exploding for 49 points in a game 1 loss, then a playoff-record 63 points in a game 2 defeat. To best describe how sublime Jordan's 63-point act was, Bird said, "It was God disguised as Michael Jordan." Despite Jordan's high-scoring outputs, the Bulls were no match for the Celtics. The series was over in three although Jordan did average 43.7 ppg for the series. The Celtics steamed past the Hawks and MVP finalist Dominique Wilkins in five, then steamrolled the Bucks in the conference finals in four. The Celtics held their end of the bargaining, What about the Lakers? The Lakers went 62-20 (second-best behind "You Know Who") and Magic (18.8 ppg, 12.6 apg, 5.9 rpg) notched another All-NBA First Team season, however the season would end in an abrupt and unexpected way. You know: getting upset in the West finals to a lesser Rockets team and losing game 5 at The Forum on a preposterous buzzer-beater by Ralph Sampson. Utter disbelief for L.A. (I still can't believe they lost to Houston. Yes, the Twin Towers of Sampson and Hakeem presented problems for them but overall L.A. was a more complete team. There's a good reason why the Lakers won 11 more games than the Rockets. They were better. A third consecutive Lakers-Celtics Finals would have been fond). In an anticlimactic finals, the Celtics handled the Rockets in six games to cap off what is considered the best NBA team of all-time. Bird was named Finals MVP for the second time in his career, averaging 24.0 ppg, 9.7 rpg, and 9.5 apg for the series, including a triple-double (29 points, 12 assists, 11 rebounds) in the game 6 clincher. Already through the first seven seasons of Birds career, he had fulfilled a resume that many players would only dream of having: 3 titles, 3 MVPs, 2 Finals MVPs, 7-time All-NBA First Team and Rookie of the Year. Yup, I say things were going pretty well for Mr. Bird.

UPPER HAND: This has to go to Bird. Jordan was on the rise but not in the superstar category quite yet. Magic got the Lakers to 60-plus wins and had a typical A+ season, yet Birds play, season, and impact was above Magic's. The Hick from French Lick was in a zone and at the zenith of his ability. Well in front **BIRD**.

1987: What a year 1987 turned out to be for this threesome! In all estimate, Bird, Magic and Jordan might have had the finest seasons of their entire career in '87. Jordan's performance this season catapulted him to superstar status. MJ went nuts and averaged an outlandish league and career high 37.1 ppg (the sixth highest scoring average for a season in NBA history) on .48% shooting joining, Wilt Chamberlain as the only players to score 3,000 points or more in a season (3,041), and became the first player to have 200 steals and 100 blocks in a season. Talk about budding into a superstar! Bird possibly had the best statistical season of his life (averaging 28.1 ppg, 9.2 rpg, 7.6 apg) and became the first player in NBA history to reach the 50-40-90 Club milestone (50 percent field goal percentage, 40 percent from three-point line, 90 percent from free throw line) in one season, and led the Celtics to 59 wins, good for a No. 1 seed in the East. In the unequivocal premier season of his career, Magic took his game up a remarkable level. For years, Magic had been the second scoring option behind Kareem and sometimes the third behind Worthy but due to Kareem's aging and diminishing gracefully, Magic became the primary offensive option and seized control of the Lakers as the main alpha dog. He averaged a career-high 23.9 ppg, a league-leading 12.2 apg, 6.3 rpg, and led L.A. to an NBA-high 65 wins. Geez, I can't think of any NBA season where three players played at the high level that MJ, Larry and Magic played at in '87. In a terrific MVP race (maybe the best ever), Magic finished first, MJ second and Bird third. Yep, doesn't get any better than that! In the first round, Jordan and Bird battled again, with the Celtics besting the Bulls again in a sweep. Bird guided the injury-riddled Celtics back to the Finals getting through two rough, demanding seven-game series past the Milwaukee Bucks and Detroit Pistons. Meanwhile the Lakers were in cruise control out West, freewheeling into the Finals at 11-1. The Lakers and Celtics met in the finals for the third and final time in the '80s, and with both teams tied with three NBA crowns for the decade, the winner would jump ahead and take the lead. The Lakers would take that lead, beating the C's 4-2 for their fourth championship of the decade. Magic's defining moment of the series and probably his career was the game-winning junior sky hook he made in the game 4 victory at Boston Garden. The Celtics injuries caught up to them and the much younger Lakers served up too much firepower. Bird's (24.2 ppg, 10.0 rpg, 5.5 apg) play for the series was particularly stout but Magic's (26.2 ppg, 13.0 apg, 8.0 rpg, 2.3 spg) game rose to perennial prestige in the series, winning his third Finals MVP. Magic called the '87 team his best Lakers team and most people agree. They could shoot it well, rebound well, had athleticism, possessed a devastating inside-outside attack and their fast-break game was bar none at its peak. (I'm going to slightly disagree with Magic. I'm riding with the '85 Lakers as the best Showtime team. They were deeper, more talented (Kareem, Worthy, Magic, Scott, McAdoo, Cooper, Wilkes, Rambis, McGee), Kareem in '85 was much better than Kareem in '87, they had the highest team field goal percentage (54.5%) and assists per game average (31.4) of any team in history. Call me crazy but I'm rolling with the '85 squad). It couldn't have been more salivating for Magic to topple his fiercest rival in another championship series and things would only look up from here.

UPPER HAND: All three had unbelievable years, however Magic's transformation from pass-first, versatile, do-it-all playmaker into a more offensive-minded, take charge, still elite passer and all-around player mode was truly riveting to behold. Magic's overall body of work in '87 tips the scale over Bird and Jordan. After the Lakers clinched the series in game 6, Bird looking dejected at a press conference stated, "Magic is a great, great basketball player. The best I've ever seen." That's all that needs to be said. Getting props like that from your biggest rival (whether they meant it or not) is high praise. It was the year of **MAGIC.**

1988: At this point going into the '88 season, it was clear who the three best players in the NBA were. Magic, Jordan and Bird together had separated themselves from the rest of the pack. Players like Hakeem, Barkley, K. Malone, Ewing, Wilkins, Isiah and Drexler were looking through the rearview window back at the trio. Not only was Jordan turning into a global icon because of his play on the court, but he became the first athlete to go mainstream in the on and off the field/court facets of the game in media and marketing. The Nike brand of his "Air Jordan" shoes/apparel/equipment has, still is, and will always be desirable to the public and a worldwide magnetism. Jordan's '88 campaign has to go down as one of the most historic, all-around individual seasons in NBA history. It was imperative that Michael Jeffrey Jordan wasn't going to be stopped. He led the league in scoring with 35.0 ppg on .53% shooting, dished out 5.9 apg, pulled down 5.5 rpg, blocked 1.6 shots a game, averaged a league-high 3.16 spg, and won about every major honor: Most Valuable Player, Defensive Player of the Year (first and only player to win the scoring title and Defensive Player of the Year in the same season), All-NBA First Team, All-Defensive First Team, All-Star Game MVP (scored 40 points in front of the home city Chicago fans), was the Slam Dunk Champion for the second year in a row, and led the Bulls to 50 wins only to be exited out by the Pistons in the second round. Good Lawd! The only thing he didn't do was win the title. Bird and Magic were again up to their old sizzling tricks. Bird (MVP runner-up) threw up a career high 29.9 ppg, along with 9.3 rpg, 6.1 apg (another 50-40-90 year) on .52% shooting, .41% from three-point line, .91% from free throw line and helped the Celtics secure the No. 1 seed in the East for the fifth straight season. Magic & Co. faced a ton of pressure coming into the season, mainly from head coach Pat Riley (Michael Douglas look-alike) guaranteeing his team will repeat during their '87 championship celebration – a feat no team had accomplished in 19 years since the Celtics in 1968-69. Riley's team was up to the task and Magic (third place in the MVP voting) would be the one leading the charge, getting the Lakers to an NBA-best 62-20 on averages of 19.6 ppg, 11.9 apg, and 6.2 rpg. The Lakers reached the Finals, surviving two seven-game wars against the Utah Jazz and Dallas Mavericks. There they met the New Kids on the Block in the "Bad Boy" Pistons, who took out Bird and the Celtics in the conference finals in six games. In a physical, grinding seven-game series, the Lakers prevailed at the heels of Finals MVP James Worthy's incredible game 7 (36 points, 16 rebounds, 10 assists) and Magic's (21.1 ppg, 13.0 apg, 5.7 rpg Finals average) steady guidance and well-rounded play. With back-to-back titles and a total of five NBA championships won in the decade, the Showtime Lakers cemented themselves as the "NBA Team of the '80s" and no player was more responsible for the Lakers success than Earvin "Magic" Johnson.

UPPER HAND: It was another insanely good 1-2-3 MVP race between the three if I might say, yet as wonderful as Bird was, this comes down to MJ and Magic. Like I said, the only thing Jordan didn't do this season was win the title. Everything else he achieved. The dude went bananas in '88. With his fifth title, another virtuoso season and almost certainly having asserted himself as the "Best NBA Player of the '80s" (with Bird at a close second), how could you not go with Magic here. Ladies and Gentleman, I usually don't do this (matter of fact I haven't done this yet throughout my list) but you've given me no choice. Magic and Jordan were both just too impressive to distinguish one from the other. **MAGIC** and **JORDAN** in a split.

1989: Unfortunately for Bird, he would only participate in six games for the year due to undergoing surgery to remove bone spurs in the back of both his heels. Without Bird, the Celtics slipped radically all the way from the No. 1 seed a year ago to the paltry No. 8 seed and were pounced in the first round by the hungry Pistons. Magic and the two-time defending champion Lakers came into the season amped for an opportunity at a three-peat. At this stage in his career, Magic kept redefining the point guard position and continued upping the level of how it should be played, and folks... nobody was close to playing point guard the way Magic was playing it. He submitted another fine season (averaging 22.5 ppg on .50% shooting, 12.8 apg, 7.9 rpg), added his second MVP trophy to his collection and led the Lake Show to a West-best 57 wins. Jordan on the hand had a totally surreal season. Air Jordan's '89 performance was the best all-around season of his career (league-leading 32.5 ppg, 10th in the NBA and a career-high 8.0 apg, career-high 8.0 rpg, and 3rd in the league in steals at 2.8 per game) and possibly the best season a two-guard has ever had. At the time, no player put up numbers like that since Oscar in the early/mid '60s. He finished as the MVP runner-up and led an average Bulls team that was making considerable strides to the top to 47 wins and an impressive run to the East finals, only to be defeated by the Bad Boy Pistons. Jordan averaged 34.8 ppg in 17 postseason games and one of the major highlights of his career was the memorable buzzer-beater jumper (*The Shot*) he hit over Craig Ehlo in the pivotal game 5 road win versus the Cleveland Cavaliers in the first round. Magic and the Lakers crew prolonged their Western dominance by smoking through the West bracket 11-0 and back into the Finals. In a rematch with the Pistons and Magic's good friend Isiah Thomas, things did not go as planned. Injuries would play a major part in the series for L.A. as they were without shooting guard Bryon Scott for the entire series and Magic suffered a hamstring injury in game 2 that knocked him out the rest of the game. Magic tried to play through the pain in game 3, but he only lasted for five minutes before going out the game and didn't play the rest of the series. It appeared to be the Pistons time and they won the title in a sweep. It was the great Kareem Abdul-Jabbar's last game and it was a difficult defeat for Magic and the Lakers to swallow.

UPPER HAND: The obvious choice here is either Magic or Jordan. Magic won the MVP. Jordan was the runner-up. Magic got his team to the Finals for the eighth time in his career. Jordan led his inferior squad to the conference finals. Both had great, all-around seasons, were the preeminent players at their position by a long shot, and were the two main marketing draws on and off the court. I really can't pick one over the other in this circumstance, even if I wanted to. I'm doing it again my lovely readers. **JORDAN** and **MAGIC** in another tie.

1990: Bird returned for the Celtics to average 24.3 ppg, 9.5 rpg, and 7.5 apg but continuous back problems and an aging roster prevented Boston from being serious title threats like usual. Their 52 wins were good for a No. 4 seed, although they were sent home by a rising Knicks team in the first round in five games. Jordan and Magic were at it again playing tug-a-war for the "league's best superstar." Without Kareem, the Lakers were not as great but with the main core of Worthy-Scott-

Cooper-Thompson-Green still intact and Kareem's new replacement, Vlade Divac adjusting well, they were still championship contenders -- going an NBA-best 63-19. Mr. Johnson was never better, winning his third MVP award in which he put up 22.3 ppg, 11.5 apg, 6.6 rpg in the regular season and became the all-time assist leader surpassing Oscar Robertson. In Chicago, things were starting to look up for the surging Bulls as they began climbing into the upper echelon of the league. Led by Jordan, under new head coach, Phil Jackson's complex Triangle Offense and the improvement of Scottie Pippen and Horace Grant, the Bulls raced to a 55-27 record. MJ (third place in the MVP voting) was once again superb, winning the scoring title at 33.6 ppg, along with 6.9 rpg, 6.3 apg, and a league-leading 2.7 spg. He even scored a career-high 69 points against the Cavaliers during the season. In the playoffs, Jordan guided the Bulls on a strong run past the Bucks and Sixers into the conference finals versus the defending champions and the Bulls chief rival, the Bad Boy Pistons. Just as the Pistons did the following two years against Jordan in the playoffs, they kept employing their "Jordan Rules" strategy to throw two to three defenders at him when he got the ball at all times, smother him constantly and physically rough him up. The Bulls kept the series within walking distance and pushed it to a seventh game but it just wasn't their time. The Pistons won game 7 and returned to the Finals, where they were expected to meet the Lakers again for the third year in a row, but instead met the Blazers – who they defeated 4 games to 1. The top-seeded Lakers were ousted in five games to the Suns in the conference semifinals. It was their earliest playoff exit since going out in the first round in 1981.

UPPER HAND: This will be another tight finish. Jordan proved to be more effective on both sides of the ball than Magic and it showed in his play and numbers. He even carried a much weaker roster to the conference finals, even though the Bulls were on the cusp of becoming the "Next Great Team." All that is true but you can't put enough emphasis on the kind of positive effect Magic had on his teammates during the '90 season (remember Jordan was labeled as a bad teammate and a selfish player in '89 and '90). Even without Kareem, Magic still managed to win the MVP and lead the club to another 60-win season without missing a beat. His direction of the team, ability to get the most out of his teammates, how he was able to get them the ball in the best position possible to succeed and his overall command of the game stood out over what Jordan did. I call it the "Magic Effect." He just had the "IT" factor. **MAGIC** this close.

1991: It had been six seasons and the Great Michael Jordan had yet to get his team to the promise land. Many experts/critics held Jordan most accountable for the Bulls inability to win a title primarily because of his selfish ways and incapability to make his teammates better. That criticism only intensified Jordan's desire to prove them wrong. The endless notion was that a team could not win a championship built around a shooting guard (to that point championship teams were largely built around point guards and big men) and no player could both lead the league in scoring and carry their team to a title. The last player to accomplish that feat was Kareem in 1971 with the Bucks, who was named Lew Alcindor at the time. Well, Jordan (31.5 ppg, 53.9% shooting, 6.0 rpg, 5.5 apg) was on the right track to prove his naysayers wrong; leading the Bulls to the Easts top-seed at 61-21 and for the first time since he's been in Chicago, they had a legitimate shot at becoming champions. Bird's back problems continued to bother him and caused him to be in-and-out of the lineup, however that didn't interfere in a veteran, over-the-hill Boston team from carving into a 56-26 mark. The Lakers once more were in the title mix, not as formidable as the '80s teams, yet still more capable than ever of getting back to the Finals. MVP runner-up Magic (19.4 ppg, 12.5 apg, 7.0 rpg) pushed L.A. to 58 W's in the regular season and in the postseason they returned back to the Finals, upsetting the West favorite Blazers in the conference finals. For the Celtics, they were eliminated in the second round by the two-time defending champion Pistons. League MVP Jordan carried his title-worthy Bulls all the way to the Finals, along the road finally defeating their arch-nemesis Pistons in a clean sweep in the Eastern conference finals. The NBA Finals was here! Bulls vs. Lakers. Michael vs. Magic. The New Guard vs. The Old Guard. There were plenty of storylines to headline in this series and the hype would only insinuate as the series drew near. The Lakers had the championship experience and the understanding of what it took to win; but the Bulls were thirsty, yearning for a ring and overall they were the better team. After all the pitfalls and stumbles the Bulls came across for years, they could finally relax and call themselves CHAMPIONS. Jordan's (31.2 ppg, 11.4 apg, 6.6 rpg, 2.8 spg, 1.4 bpg) Finals MVP play, Pippen's active defense against Magic, and the all-out togetherness and growth of the Bulls (they went 15-2 in the playoffs) was the difference in defeating the Lakers 4-1 and claiming the franchise's first championship. In Magic's last Finals, he played well averaging 18.6 ppg, 12.4 apg, and 8.0 rpg, though MJ was not going to be denied this year. Jordan had finally silenced his critics. The torch had been passed.

UPPER HAND: No disrespect to Bird and Magic but '91 was all about Jordan. No if's, and's, and but's about it. He had at last learned how to mesh his exceptional individual gifts with his teammates and take their game to a higher level (even if he did get away from the game plan sometimes), and it did help that his teammates were greatly improved. He was in the prime of his career and on the verge of single-handedly owning the league. **JORDAN** overwhelmingly.

1992: Before the season, Magic sadly and shockingly announced that he had contracted HIV (human immunodeficiency virus), and he was forced to retire from professional basketball immediately. It wasn't just one of the most shocking and startling sports moments in sports history but also in American history. Despite his retirement, fans still voted Magic into the 1992 NBA All-Star Game in Orlando, which stirred up some controversy and seemed risky and unsafe by opposing players and his former teammates – if he decided to play. Magic decided to play and play well he did. He put on an All-Star Game performance to remember -- winning the game MVP pouring in 25 points, 9 assists, 5 rebounds, and hitting a late, deep three-pointer that sent the crowd into a frenzy. This would not be Magic's last great basketball moment. Bird's last season was a tough one as the back injuries piled up and he missed 37 games. On one last run, Bird led the Celtics to the conference semifinals but they went down to the Cavaliers in seven games with Bird missing four out of the seven games due to the recurring back problems. Meanwhile, everything was going as smooth as gravy for His Airness. Jordan (30.1 ppg, 6.4 rpg, 6.1 apg, 2.2 spg, 51 FG%) at this stage was at the pinnacle of his skill: athleticism, ultimate confidence, physically, mentally, drive to destroy anything in his path, ample of enough moves in the offensive repertoire, three-point game, defensive intensity through the roof, and a better understanding of balancing when to take over and when to get his teammates involved. Jordan won his second consecutive MVP and carried the Bulls to the NBA's top record at 67-15, and were clear favorites to win it all again. The Bulls playoff run wasn't as undemanding as a year ago, yet they managed to get back to the Finals after winning a burdensome 7-game war over the Knicks and a physical 6-game series over the Cavs. In the championship round, Jordan and the Bulls met MVP runner-up Clyde Drexler and the West-best Portland Trail Blazers. The talk going in was that Drexler was just as good as Jordan and maybe even better. MJ squashed that argument quick. In game 1, Mike scored a Finals-record 35 points in the first half, including a record-tying six 3-pointers in the half. This was the famous, "Shrug Game" people, one of the best moments of his career. The Bulls won game 1 and they eventually won the series 4-2 to win back-to-back crowns. Jordan (35.8 ppg, 4.8 rpg, 6.5 apg) won his second Finals MVP and the championships were soon to pile up for the "NBA's Best Player."

UPPER HAND: This needs no explanation. **JORDAN.**

Looks like Magic had the Upper Hand 5 times, Jordan 4 times, and Bird twice. Attention-grabbing or what. I would say so. Nothing knocks getting a year-by-year edge over your biggest rivals and competition.

- This fact is very worthy of note: From 1984 to 1992, either Jordan, Bird or Magic took home the MVP (Jordan 3, Bird 3, Magic 3). One word: Ridiculous!

Who would have ever thunk it! In the summer of 1992, the three greatest players of their generation/era together joined the USA Olympic Team called "The Dream Team" along with other NBA stars to compete in the Olympics in Barcelona, Spain. Heading into the Olympics, Jordan was enjoying his prime, while the older, past-their-prime, still efficient Bird and Magic were rolling along. The minute the games started the three put on a show, created highlight reel after highlight reel, and helped guide the U.S. team to the gold medal in dominant style. It was an experience they'll never forget. Bird retired after the Olympics and later became head coach for the Indiana Pacers -- winning Coach of the Year in 1998 and ledg Indiana to the NBA Finals in 2000, only to fall to (that's right) the Lakers. Magic did a little bit of everything: became an HIV/AIDS spokesperson, author, businessman, color commentator for NBC Sports, hosted a late-night talk show called *The Magic Hour* for a couple of months, had a brief stint as the Lakers head coach in 1994 and made a comeback with the Lakers as a power forward for 32 games (14.6 ppg, 6.9 apg, 5.7 rpg) in the 1996 season before retiring for good at season's end. Jordan sustained his dominance on the league throughout the '90s, winning his third title and third Finals MVP in '93; then retired to play minor league baseball; but he returned to the Bulls in 1995, and went along to win three more titles (1996-1998), two more MVP awards (1996, 1998), three more Finals MVPs (1996-1998), two more All-Star Game MVPs (1996, 1998), three more scoring titles (1996-1998), and made three more First Teams (1996-1998). Jordan retired in '98, then later made another comeback with the Washington Wizards from 2001-2003, before wrapping it up for good. Three Legends at work!

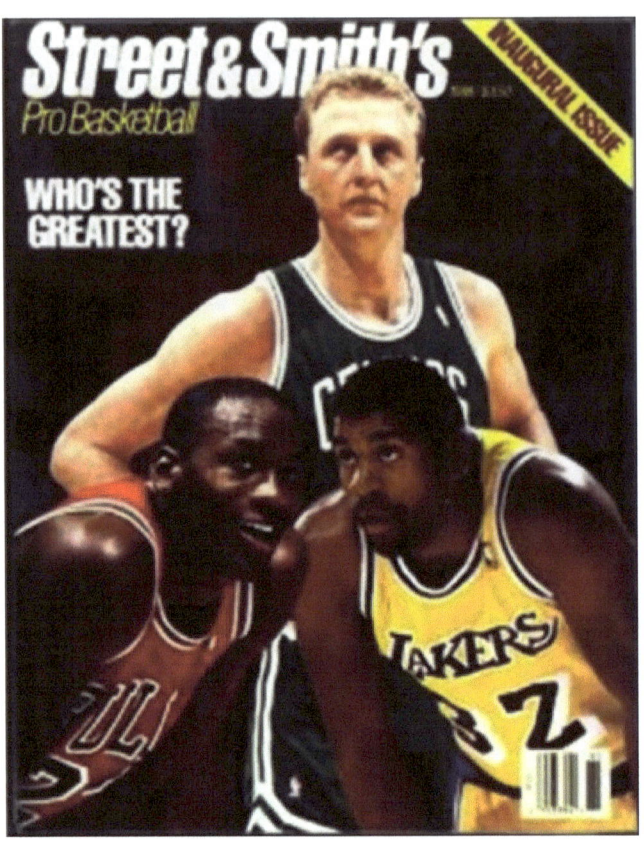

The Debate was ranging more than ever in 1988.

Boxing out during the 1985 NBA Finals.

Bird and Jordan squaring off.

Air Jordan soaring through the air, while Magic looks on.

Larry and Magic: Maybe the greatest sports dispute ever.

Matching up at the 1987 All-Star Game.

The rings are the thing. Just ask Mike.

The Holy Trinity on one team. That ain't fair at all.

So, Who's Better- In my estimation, Jordan, Magic and Bird are three of the five greatest NBA players of all-time. Jordan the greatest shooting guard, Bird the greatest small forward and Magic the greatest point guard. No question about it. Their pro careers speak for themselves...

MAGIC- 5 NBA Championships, 3 MVPs, 2-time MVP runner-up, 3 Finals MVPs, 12-time NBA All-Star, 2 All-Star Game MVPs, 9-time All-NBA First Team, 4-time NBA assist leader, 2-time NBA steals leader, 2nd all-time in triple-doubles (138), Member of NBAs 50th Anniversary All-Time Team, Best season in my opinion: 1987

    Career averages: 19.5 ppg, 11.2 apg (1st all-time), 7.2 rpg
    Playoff averages: 19.5 ppg, 12.3 apg (1st all-time), 7.7 rpg

BIRD- 3 NBA Championships, 3 MVPS, 4-time MVP runner-up, 2 Finals MVP, 12-time NBA All-Star, 1 All-Star Game MVP, Rookie of the Year, 9-time All-NBA First Team, 3-time All-Defensive Second Team, 3-time Three-Point Shootout Champion, Member of NBAs 50th Anniversary All-Time Team, Best season in my opinion: 1986

    Career averages: 24.3 ppg, 10.0 rpg, 6.3 apg
    Playoff averages: 23.8 ppg, 10.3 rpg, 6.5 apg

JORDAN- 6 NBA Championships, 5 MVPs, 3-time MVP runner-up, 6 Finals MVP, 14-time NBA All-Star, 3-time NBA All-Star Game MVP, 10-time All-NBA First Team, 10-time All-Defensive First Team, Rookie of the Year, Defensive Player of the Year, 10 scoring titles, 3-time NBA steals leader, 2-time Slam Dunk Contest Champion, Member of NBAs 50th Anniversary All-Time Team, Best season in my opinion: Undetermined

    Career averages: 30.1 ppg (1st all-time), 6.2 rpg, 5.3 apg
    Playoff averages: 33.4 ppg (1st all-time), 6.4 rpg, 5.7 apg

It's hard to say whose career was better because each of their legacies are equally remarkable and celebrated in the history of basketball, and will be decades from now.

One interesting topic: When I covered their career achievements, I noted what I thought each player's best season was. Magic's '87 and Bird's '86 seasons stand out to me as their best. They each won the MVP, Finals MVP, put up all-around numbers and both played on their best championship teams, as many considered. Now you ask -- What was Jordan's best season? Good luck choosing com padre. Asking what Michael Jordan's best season is like asking what Elvis' best song was (he has the third most No. 1 hits of all-time with 17, the second most top 10 singles at 36 and the most top 40 hits at 104) or asking to name Katharine Hepburn's best performance on the big screen (the gal was selected for 12 Academy Award nominations for Best Actress and won a record 4 times – the most ever by a male or female performer). It's impossible to pick but I'm going to try. The years that stick out for Jordan are: '87, '88, '89, '91, '92, '96, and '98. If I had to pick one, then '96 would be my choice. MJ wasn't at his peak athletically and didn't have the explosion like he used to but he adjusted his game to becoming more physical, resourceful, smarter, understanding the team concept better, and relied more heavily on experience, will, leadership, and determination. Plus, he won the regular season MVP, All-Star Game MVP, Finals MVP all in the same season (only three players in NBA history have done that: Willis Reed in 1970, Jordan in 1996 and 1998, and Shaquille O'Neal in 2000) and led the Bulls to the best record in league history (72-10), along with winning the title. The man did it all that year!

To determine who was better between Bird and Magic, well all you have to do is look back at the Bird-Johnson-Erving section where I picked Magic over Bird because I felt he carried his team better throughout his career than Bird did during his career. Now if you wanna converse in who's superior over the other at certain skills/categories, then let's hit it in full stride:

Better Shooter- I always thought Magic was a better shooter than people gave him credit for being. In the mid-'80s, he became a very good mid-range shooter, added range in the late-'80s/early '90s to evolve as a solid 3-point shooter, was a reliable free throw shooter, and shot .52% from the field for his career. Saying all that, Bird was not only the better shooter, but in my opinion – the best ever: three-point, mid-range, free throws, face ups, turnaround, catch-and-shoot, and runners with either hand. First 50-40-90 club member. Bird's greatest basketball attribute was his shooting ability. Yep, he could shoot it from anywhere, at anytime. EDGE: BIRD.

Offense- Bird has a higher career average (24.3) than Magic (19.5), although when Magic was asked to carry the offensive load more, his numbers jumped to around 23-24 per game. Don't let the 19 per game fool you. Bird wasn't the fastest or the most athletic, however he got his from the inside and outside: spotting up to shoot, coming off screens/curls to get easy points in the paint, quick transition buckets, posting up and putbacks off offensive rebounds. Bird couldn't create his shot as well as the likes of Jordan, Kobe, and Dr. J; yet his scrappy, hardworking mentality was what propelled him into being a well-rounded offensive player. One word to describe Magic's offensive game: Versatile. Magic is the only player in NBA history (maybe Kevin Garnett) that can play all five positions and play them all effectively well. With his 6'9" frame, he was more unique than any player we've ever seen. The "Master of Creativity" is what Magic was. He posted up well (perfected the baby hook he used later in his career), was a marvelous penetrator (especially on a coast-to-coast fast break), had a solid runner/leaner, great spin moves, excellent change of direction/pace, and occasionally if caught sleeping he would slam one home on you. Magic was quicker, a better ball-handler, more athletic and could put the ball in the basket in more ways than Bird could. EDGE: MAGIC.

Rebounder- Tough to choose. In their playing days, they each were the best rebounder at their respective positions. Bird grinded, battled and positioned himself to rebound better than any small forward maybe ever (can't forget about Elgin Baylor). Magic was always around the basket, getting the defensive rebound like a power forward and pushing the ball at will. To me, Magic was a more natural rebounder; but Bird had, to some extent, a better knack for the ball. Also, Magic did have a ton of huge rebounding games in his career, although Bird happened to have a little bit more bigger games cleaning the glass. EDGE: BIRD.

Passer- The Best Debate of them all! Magic is the greatest point guard passer of all-time, while Bird is the greatest small forward passer of all-time. Both of their passing was unlike anything the league had ever witnessed. It was exciting, thrilling, addicting, contiguous and mind-blowing to us. Kids would go to the courts, play in pickup games and have the mindset of passing rather than scoring. Why? Because Bird and Magic made it look cool and fun. If you wanna break it down carefully...They both had flair and were flashy. Bird was a better two-handed passer. Magic was a better one-handed passer. Bird was better in the half-court. Magic was better in the full-court. Bird was a better chest passer. Magic was the better alley-oop passer. To break the ice, what separated Magic from Bird in my mind was that he could make a greater number of passes in a more variety of ways. Magic was a cut above Larry at driving-and-kicking, penetrating to draw the defense to dish inside, passing from the post, his passing angles were unreal and his vision was unparallel. Overall, Magic was a greater facilitator. The best passer ever. EDGE: MAGIC.

Defense- This wasn't either player's strong suit as many point out. Both were weak one-on-one defenders and could get exposed mightily, although both excelled at team defense. Bird's anticipation to read where opponents wanted to go with the ball stood out (particularly in his early days) and Magic did a good job positioning and rotating in half-court sets. People forget that Magic led the league in steals twice ('81 and '82) but Bird's three All-Defense Team selections (all second teams) to Magic's zero All-Defense Team appearances give him the nod. EDGE: BIRD.

So there: Bird-3 and Magic-2. Let the debate continue to rage.

The million-dollar question that I have to ask...Who would you build your team/franchise around: Bird, Jordan or Magic? If I did a worldwide poll asking this question, then I'm pretty sure Jordan would be the consensus pick. Right? So you're reading this and probably saying "If it's so clear-cut, then why is this guy asking this question?" Answer: It might be clear-cut to *you* and most likely to the whole sports world but not for Mr. Simpson here. I think it's a debate and I mean a *plausible debate* too. Look, Jordan was one of those once-in-a-lifetime athletes that we will be telling our children and grandchildren about from generation to generation. Watching Jordan was like watching Shakespeare direct a play or watching Michelangelo paint the Sistine Chapel. To millions, it was like a dreamlike creation being revealed right in front of our eyes. The only thing we had to do was watch and enjoy. There was some kind of mystique and aura about MJ that only a handful of people throughout world history carried. Jordan joins the company of larger-than-life figures like Nelson Mandela, John F. Kennedy, Michael Jackson, Elvis Presley, Muhammad Ali, The Beatles, Marilyn Monroe, FDR (Franklin Delano Roosevelt), Princess Diana, Oprah, etc. He was the fiercest competitor, the hardest worker, athletically from another planet, a ferocious killer instinct to annihilate his competition and in most viewer's opinion the greatest clutch performer of all-time (with Bird and Kobe right in the mix). Air Jordan was all that and a bag of chips but I'm starting my team with Mr. Showtime. As great as Jordan was, he never made his teammates better or took them to a higher level the way that Magic and Bird did. He just didn't. He figured it out when he started winning championships but only then. Magic and Larry understood from Day One the value of not just elevating their play but also their teammates play (whether average or All-Star caliber teammates) in order to reach the ultimate goal of winning championships. When your teammates are struggling, encourage them and let them know you have their back. Build them up to be bigger and better than what they actually are. Get in their face when they make a mistake but don't kill their confidence level. Be that positive influence, provide the headstrong leadership and set the rightful example to move forward in the right direction. Bird and Magic did all those things. It came second nature to them. Jordan not so much.

To refute that you will say, "How could Jordan have made his teammates better in his early years when he played with garbage compared to Magic and Bird playing with future Hall of Famers?" In Jordan's first six years, he did play with second-rate teammates but he didn't attempt to mesh his incredible skills and talent to blend in with the team. Yeah, Jordan's teammates were nowhere close to his level and that's why the Bulls went home early every year. Although I would argue, that even if Jordan played with some All-Stars from 1984-1990, that he still wouldn't have led his team to the mountaintop. Why? Because he still *didn't* fully understand the value of team, chemistry, cohesiveness and putting teammates in the best position possible to succeed (Phil Jackson played a huge part in instilling the team concept into Jordan). Plus, even if MJ's Bulls were a championship-type squad in his first six years – they were not beating Bird's Celtics and Magic's Lakers teams in a seven-game series in the postseason and critics would have maligned him even more for not beating his main rivals, who were called "winners" while Jordan was being dubbed as a "selfish player who will never figure it out." The Lakers and Celtics were just too stacked, loaded and more of a complete team. (And if you're asking me if the Bulls of the '90s (6 titles) are better than the Lakers and Celtics of the '80s (8 titles combined in 10 years when they played in a way stronger, deeper decade) then your answer is NO – they're not. But hey, that's for a whole other discussion). For me, Magic is the perfect player to start a team with because he has all the qualities I'm looking for: has great size, can dominant all five positions, will fill the stat sheet up every night as an automatic triple-double threat (more prone to get a triple-double than Bird and Jordan), a spirited, natural-born leader, a positive/great teammate to play with, and no player in NBA history made his teammates better than Magic. You can pick Jordan but I'm taking Magic and I feel pretty damn good about it.

The Jordan-Magic debate goes something like this: Maybe the Greatest Individual Player vs. Maybe the Greatest Team Player. Best NBA Player of the '80s vs. Best NBA Player of the '90s. Selfish vs. Unselfish. One of the Best Scorers of all-time vs. One of the Best All-Around Specimen of all-time. More debatable than you realize, wouldn't you say. Magic is my guy, yet I would be an idiot to forget what Jordan did on the court (or through the air). The guy that many thought would never be a champion or much less become the champion that Magic and Bird were – proved us all wrong. Jordan defied conventional wisdom that a scoring champion (a scoring champion at the two-guard position at that) could not carry their team to a championship. (All six of Jordan's championships he won, he was the scoring champion). He won more championships, more MVPs (won 5 but should have won 6 in my book), more Finals MVPs, made more First Teams than Magic and Bird, and was far better on both the offensive and defensive side of the ball (one of the top five greatest two-way players in NBA history). Those are all deciding influences but what really separates Jordan from both his rivals are the immaculate playoff credentials he holds. His performances and moments will stand the test of time:

1986 First Round, Game 2- NBA playoff-record 63 points at Boston Garden

1988 First Round, Game 5- "The Shot" over Ehlo to win the series.

1991 NBA Finals, Game 2- "The hang in the air, switch the ball from right to left hand layup" vs. the Lakers.

1992 NBA Finals, Game 1- "The Shrug" game where he hit six 3-pointers in the first half.

1993 NBA Finals- averaged an absurd, out-of-his-mind, gets overlooked Finals record 41.0 ppg for the series, to go along with 8.5 rpg and 6.3 apg, including a 55-point evisceration in game 4. Easily, the greatest individual finals performance in NBA history.

1996 NBA Finals- in his least-impressive Finals he averaged 27.3 ppg, 5.3 rpg, 4.2 apg, and clinched the title for the 72-win '96 Bulls for having the "Greatest NBA Season of All-Time" (although I'd still go with the '72 Lakers but hey that's just my opinion).

1997 NBA Finals, Game 1- buzzer-beater over Russell; Game 5- "The Flu Game." Averaged 32.3 ppg, 7.0 rpg, 6.0 apg for the series.

1998 NBA Finals, Game 6- "The slight push-off and the Shot" again over Russell and the 45-point title-clincher. Averaged 33.5 ppg, 4.0 rpg, 2.3 apg for the series.

Another great performance after another. He never ceased to amaze us. Jordan always elevated his game on the biggest stage to renowned heights better than anyone and it resulted into two 3-peats – and as everyone constantly mentions, he and the Bulls could have won 8 titles in a row, if he didn't retire to play baseball. Don't get me wrong, Magic and Birds postseason success and performances were outstanding and memorable, however, Jordan's were a degree better. When it's all said and done, Magic was a better leader, a greater teammate, made his teammates better, I'd rather play with Magic and build a team around him but taking everything into account – Jordan was better. He just is.

My Rankings

1. **Michael Jordan**
2. **Magic Johnson**
3. **Larry Bird**

www.ingramcontent.com/pod-product-compliance
Lightning Source LLC
Chambersburg PA
CBHW040052160426
43192CB00002B/45